D1285293

Beyond the Screen:

Chinese Furniture
of the
16th and 17th Centuries

Beyond the Screen:

Chinese Furniture
of the
16th and 17th Centuries

Nancy Berliner

with contributions by

Craig Clunas

Curtis Evarts

Sarah Handler

Wang Zhengshu

Museum of Fine Arts

Boston

Copyright © 1996 by
Museum of Fine Arts
Boston, Massachusetts
All Rights Reserved

Library of Congress Cat. Card No. 96-75974
ISBN 0-87846-434-4 (cloth)
ISBN 0-87846-435-2 (paper)

Printed in the U.S.A.
by Acme Printing Co.
Wilmington, Massachusetts
Designed by Carl Zahn and
typeset in Gill Sans Alt. 1 (Monotype)

The exhibition opened at the Museum of
Fine Arts in specially designed new galleries
May 17, 1996.

Cover and frontispiece Illustration:
Cat. 1. Screen [*pingfeng*]

Table of Contents

Foreword

It is with the greatest pleasure that the Museum of Fine Arts, home of the finest collections of Asian art in the world, presents "Beyond the Screen: Chinese Furniture of the 16th and 17th Centuries." This exhibition focuses on the function and placement of the furniture in a domestic setting; the social, cultural, and philosophical context in which the furniture was designed, created, and used; and the fine craftsmanship evident in its construction techniques. Such furniture and the related decorative arts would have been part of furnishings of bedrooms, studies, and grand halls of officials and other prominent members of late Ming society, which is considered to be the golden age of Chinese furniture-making.

The Museum of Fine Arts is deeply grateful to the private collectors whose generous loans have made this important exhibition possible, as well as to The Nelson-Atkins Museum of Art, Kansas City, and the Yenching Library at Harvard University. The Shanghai Museum has loaned an exquisite set of 16th-century miniature tomb furniture, small wooden replicas of the life-size furniture that graced 16th- and 17th-century Chinese homes.

"Beyond the Screen: Chinese Furniture of the 16th and 17th Centuries" sets its subject in its literary, historical, and architectural context. With this in mind, the set is a multistructural installation that evokes the grand courtyard compounds of the late Ming period and the life that went on there.

Malcolm Rogers
Ann and Graham Gund Director

Preface

In recent years there has been increasing interest in traditional Chinese furniture among people both in China and in the West. Consequently, a need has arisen for greater appreciation and deeper understanding of it.

By reconstructing the residential environment of the past, visitors can perceive the living conditions, the pleasure and atmosphere of ancient times as they stroll. In this way, the original essence of furniture is revealed and its function in daily life demonstrated. The best way to achieve this is by mounting exhibitions.

I am over eighty years old and regret that I am not able to participate in the design, planning, and installation of the furniture exhibition "Beyond the Screen." However, from its very initiation, I have been constantly informed of its progress, viewing pictures of the objects to be displayed and familiarizing myself with the design. I believe its method of presentation and the quality of the objects will cause it to be substantially different from any other furniture exhibition I have visited, and that it will be a great success in spreading the knowledge of Chinese furniture.

Being Chinese, I am very proud that Ming-period furniture has become recognized as a cultural heritage shared by people all over the world. At the same time, I feel sorry that we in China are far behind our Western colleagues in pursuing such an effort. I sincerely hope there will be more such exhibitions in the future to promote Chinese art, and that will also further the cultural exchange between China and other nations of the world.

Wang Shixiang, Beijing

Acknowledgments

For the magnificent examples of sixteenth- and seventeenth-century Chinese furniture that exist and inspire us today, I am daily grateful to the carpenters who constructed them and to the patrons who commissioned them. The current display of these pieces, here in Boston and in this catalogue, however, is due entirely to the encouragement, support, passion, and hard work of many other people who have persisted in bringing this exhibition and its publication to fruition.

First, I thank the many lenders who are the spiritual descendants of the first owners and commissioners of these pieces, who have taken it upon themselves to care for their present welfare, and who generously were willing to share them with the public. In addition to the private collectors, the staff and administration of two great museums—the Shanghai Museum, in Shanghai, China, and The Nelson-Atkins Museum of Art, in Kansas City, Missouri—have been extremely accommodating and generous in lending objects from their illustrious collections.

The superb and highly experienced staff at the Museum of Fine Arts, including Brent Benjamin, Bill Burback, Judy Downes, Dave Geldart, Katie Getchel, Tom Lang, Barbara Martin, Malcolm Rogers, Janice Sorkow, Tessa Virr Atkinson, John Woolf, Susan Wong, Wu Tung, and Carl Zahn, have been the foundation and principal realizers of this exhibition. Collaboration with the outside contractors who became involved in this project—the architects Yusing Jung and Joe Mamayek of Jung/Brannen Associates, who with professional experience and grace created an engaging design to exhibit the objects, and Brian Hotchkiss, whose superior editing skills and unflappable gentle manner expertly guided the refining process of this manuscript—has been a great joy. It was an honor, as well, to work with the additional contributors to this catalogue—Craig Clunas, Curtis Evarts, Sarah Handler, and Wang Zhengshu—all of whom willingly and punctually produced essays of important scholarly merit.

In researching the background information for this project and catalogue, I am particularly grateful to two great scholars in China, Zhu Jiajin and Wang Shixiang, who, over the past ten years, have frequently and readily opened the doors of their warm homes to share their knowledge and advice. Conversations through the years with the ever-ebullient and perspicacious Edward C. Johnson 3d have also been a cardinal inspiration for the exhibition and this catalogue.

Along the route toward the completion of this project, I have become indebted to many people—too numerous to list here—who have offered their expert knowledge and skills. Among them are Raoul Birnbaum, Christine Downing, the staff of Harvard Yenching and Rubel Library, Fernando Henriques, Jin Wen, William Lipton, Michael Melanson, Ross Miller, Christina Nelson, Peter Rosenberg, Richard Rosenblum, Tian Jiaqing, David Van Meter, Leon and Karen Wender, Ellen Widmer, Barbara Warren, Xie Liqiong, Yuan Quanyu, Zeng Xiaojun, and Zhu Chuanrong. Additionally, working with the most-obliging

Ma Chengyuan, Wang Qingzheng, Zhu Shuyi, Zhou Yanqun, and Wang Zhengshu of the Shanghai Museum has been a delightful experience. In Boston, Anne-Marie Soulliere's affable guidance has been invaluable. Libby Caterino's wise eyes and erudition concerning carpentry have made essential and daily contributions. Likewise, Tara Cederholm's immutable assistance, expertise, and shared enthusiasm was a cornerstone for the exhibition and this catalogue.

       The support and encouragement of close friends and family, including my parents, Barnett and Marilyn Berliner, and my life-partner Bill Mellins, are, as always, vital and cherished.

Nancy Berliner

Chronology of Chinese Dynasties and Reign Periods

Xia	21st–16th century B.C.
Shang	16th–11th century B.C.
Western Zhou	11th century–770 B.C.
Eastern Zhou	770–221 B.C.
Spring and Autumn Period	770–475 B.C.
Warring States Period	475–221 B.C.
Qin	221–207 B.C.
Western Han	206 B.C.–24 A.D.
Eastern Han	24–220 A.D.
Three Kingdoms	220–280
Western Jin	265–316
Eastern Jin	317–420
Southern and Northern Dynasties	420–589
Sui	581–618
Tang	618–906
Five Dynasties and Ten Kingdoms	907–979
Song	960–1279
Yuan	1279–1368
Ming	**1368–1644**
Hongwu	1368–1398
Jianwen	1399–1402
Yongle	1403–1424
Hongxi	1425–1425
Xuande	1426–1435
Zhengtong	1436–1449
Jingtai	1450–1456
Tianshun	1457–1464
Chenghua	1465–1487
Hongzhi	1488–1505
Zhengde	1506–1521
Jiajing	1522–1566
Longqing	1567–1572
Wanli	1573–1620
Taichang	1620–1620
Tianqi	1621–1627
Chongzhen	1628–1644
Qing	**1644–1911**
Shunzhi	1644–1661
Kangxi	1662–1722
Yongzheng	1723–1735
Qianlong	1736–1796
Jiaqing	1796–1820
Daoguang	1821–1850
Xianfeng	1851–1861
Tongzhi	1862–1874
Guangxu	1875–1908
Xuantong	1909–1911

Introduction

"The universe is vast and time is eternal"
　　　Inscription on a grand Chinese table

During the sixteenth and seventeenth century, at the end of the Ming period and the dawn of the Qing, the design and craftsmanship of Chinese furniture reached an unprecedented apex. Economic development, social mobility, a sharp rise in the interest in aesthetics, and the skills of artisans, refined over many generations, all intersected, for one elongated moment, to bring the evolution of furniture design to its full and radiant maturation. Today, over three hundred years later, the elegant restraint and gentle lines of this furniture can still move those who rest their eyes upon it.

In the presence of a fine piece of Chinese furniture, the connoisseur first stands at a distance to appreciate its general form. Slowly he approaches the object of his attention, considering its proportions; then he moves closer and studies the carving and the joinery. He checks around the side, pulls out a magnifying glass to observe any tool marks on the surface. Eventually, when no one is looking, he crawls underneath with his flashlight to view the inner structure.

Like the connoisseur, this exhibition and its accompanying catalogue attempt to look at sixteenth- and seventeenth-century Chinese furniture from as many viewpoints as possible—spatial and temporal; close and distant. A wide spatial perspective offers a view of the furniture within its architectural contexts— the rooms in which the pieces were placed, what other accouterments surrounded it, and which pieces abutted which—while closer viewpoints allow inspection of joinery and craftsmanship. A distant temporal standpoint affords an overall account of the evolution of the forms, while a closer temporal inspection ascertains the social and economic contexts of the late Ming period when the pieces were crafted. And miniature furniture found in late Ming tombs extends our view even beyond these immediate temporal and spatial milieu to the imagined life of the netherworld.

The contemporary world in which these stunning seventeenth-century pieces were created generously provided us with further artistic modalities through which to experience the furniture. Characters in the literature of the time are described as strolling among tables, sitting on stools, lounging on couch-beds, and even tossing their silk robes languidly over garment racks, all of which are situated properly in appropriate rooms. Vernacular stories as well as classical poems inform us that chairs were often brought along on trips (or thrown out windows in brawls), that incense tables were commonly carried outdoors, and that beds were convenient places under which to hide from a jealous husband.

The multitude of interiors depicted in woodblock prints from the Huizhou district of Anhui province and elsewhere also offer a sense of furniture arrangement and function during the late Ming and early Qing periods. Unfortunately, these images probably cannot be accepted as exact replicas of their contemporary environments. Their designers were working primarily within standard, formulaic compositions passed down to them by earlier artisans in the same field. Often they were merely copying those patterns. Other times, they were certainly relying on their vivid imaginations. Moreover, these designers

The four characters—*yu, zhou, hong, huang*—inscribed with ink on the interior side of the aprons of cat. 19.

arranged the furniture within the frames of their pictures to create the best stage set to display the actions of the storyline. But though these images are not reliable photographic depictions of Ming interiors, as we compare images of furniture in woodblock prints with objects found in storerooms and collections, more than a mere coincidental number of matches are seen. These printed scenes provide clues of how various types of furniture were used. Therefore, in order to present a sense of room arrangements and a feel for human interactions with furniture— were their feet up on the couch-bed's surface or did they hang down?—this text has been enhanced with excerpts from literature and woodblock-print illustrations that are contemporary with the construction of the furniture.

In contemplating Chinese furniture from all directions, the human beings for whom these objects were intended cannot be neglected. Craig Clunas, in his essay "Furnishing the Self in Early Modern China," discusses the patrons who sat on, ate at, worshiped before, and studied using the furniture; who commissioned it, occasionally designed it, and who proudly showed it off to friends and associates, in the hopes that these objects would be ambassadors of their own identities. In "The Furniture Maker and the Woodworking Traditions of China," Curtis Evarts considers the populace at the nascent moment on the lifeline of a given piece of furniture—the men who began with raw logs (or occasionally with a fellow crafts-man's end product—an existing piece of old furniture), then sawed, planed, and shaped hardwood into exquisite objects for their clients' enjoyment and comfort. Exploring how the great Ming carpenters arrived at such perfected designs, Sarah Handler, in her essay "Wood Shaped and Standing through the Winds of Time," analyzes the long development of furniture designs and their details. The lines of an apron on a table, carved by a seventeenth-century carpenter, could be echoes of a bronzeworker's design from more than two millennia before. Finally, Wang Zhengshu investigates the knowledge about furniture styles and furniture arrange-ment that may be distilled from an examination of the fine, miniature wooden fur-niture found in the tomb of a late-Ming official.

Furniture was never as exalted an artform as painting, or even as porce-lain. Ming painters often wrote long inscriptions on their works describing the moods or occasions for which the work was produced, and imperial porcelain craftsmen at least marked the reign period on the bases of their works. However, artisans creating furniture during that time period were never so eloquent or pro-lific with the written language. Rarely did Ming furniture artisans even sign or date their pieces. In fact, no known piece of sixteenth- or seventeenth-century furniture has an artisan's signature or seal, and only a few have inscribed dates.[1] However, when one searches with magnifying glass and powerful flashlight, other marks and written clues left by these fine carpenters do become apparent and begin to inform. Crawling under dusty tables and chairs with a moistened rag, for instance, can reveal numerous inked characters telling short but instructive tales about the assembling of the furniture. On legs, aprons, and inside the joins of tables and chairs brush-written characters may be discerned, some elegant, some miswritten, and some even carved into the wood to imitate brushstrokes, placed there to assist the original carpenters, and possibly later reassemblers, with putting the pieces together in the proper configuration. Prosaic inscriptions, such as "front right leg" or "rear left leg" originally had an exclusively pragmatic function, but now observation of consistency of calligraphy on all parts of a piece immeasurably aids in the authentication of its entirety.

On occasion, table legs are distinguished not by position or a number, but by one of a series of characters. Sets of furniture, as well as individual legs, were "numbered" with these character series.

As noted by H. A. Giles over a century ago, a series of characters commonly used by carpenters is derived from the first sentence of an ancient and popular calligraphic exercise text, "Qian Zi Wen" (Thousand-Character Essay).[2] The variety of the text's characters made it ideal for practicing and displaying calligraphic proficiency. The first characters of the essay read "tian di xuan huang" (the heavens were dark and the earth was yellow). Often, just the first two characters, *tian* and *di*, are used to distinguish the respective parts from a pair of objects. One leg and its corresponding mortise may be labeled "tian yi" (heaven one), while a leg on the sister stool would be labeled "di yi" (earth one). In the course of disassembling many pieces of furniture, other word series have surfaced. The words on each of the four legs of one table in a private American collection read "kong shang da ren" (Kong—or Confucius—is a superior man). Three legs of another, also in a private American collection, say "Huang shang da" (Huang is superior), while its fourth leg is blank.

While these assembly markings had a practical function for the carpenter's process, the adages possibly also served as auspicious wishes for the patron's family. Klaas Ruitenbeek has pointed out that carpenters were considered to be capable of manipulating magical powers through the charms they might place in a client's new home.[3] An elderly carpenter in Hong Kong relabeled the corners of a daybed in a private American collection with characters written with Magic Marker on tape for a client planning to disassemble the piece. He explained that the characters were a series of words that had been passed down to him by his master. The phrase "jin yu man tang" (may your hall be filled with gold and jade) is clearly a wish intended for the one who would lay upon the bed.

The characters *yu zhou hong huang,* meaning "the universe is vast and time is eternal"—mark the four leg tenons and the four mortise holes into which they fit on the bottom of the long table with everted flanges in catalogue number 19. The four-character saying is the second sentence in the "Thousand-Character Essay." While the sentence may have been chosen from the text as a matter of course, it probably was also attractive as an invocation that future descendants of the client be as extensive as the universe, and as eternal as time.

The sentence can also be understood in another sense. While the moment of creation of a piece of furniture is singular, the moments of observation of it through time and space are infinite in number. A variety of time and space "lines" that follow the evolution of a design or the tastes of the patron all converged at one moment, at one place—the production of a specific piece. But the elegant seventeenth-century results presented here are not the end of those temporal and spatial trajectories. Chinese furniture was exported to Europe, and European furniture design of the eighteenth- and nineteenth-centuries was, in turn, highly influenced by it. During the first half of the twentieth century, Europeans further noticed the less-rococo aspects of Ming-style Chinese furniture, and absorbed that sophisticated refinement into their designs. Now, in 1996, the celebration of these elegant pieces at the Museum of Fine Arts, Boston, will permit them, perchance, again to have an impact on the sensibilities of beholders, and to enrich aesthetic experiences.

Notes:

1. A large, *tieli*-wood, recessed-leg table with everted flanges at the Palace Museum (Beijing) has engraved on the bottom surface of the tabletop: "Made in the mid-winter of the Gengchen year of Chongzhen [1640] at the Kang district [in Guangdong province] government office." (Wang Shixiang, *Connoisseurship of Chinese Furniture*. Trans. by Sarah Handler and the author. Hong Kong: Joint Publishing, 1990, vol. 1, p. 65.) A recessed-leg, *huanghuali* painting table at the Nanjing Museum was inscribed by its owner in 1595. See catalogue number 17.

2. H. A. Giles "Thousand-Character Numerals Used by Artisan," *Journal of the Royal Asiatic Society*, China Branch, 20 (1885), p. 279.

3. Klaas Ruitenbeek, *Carpentry and Building in Late Imperial China*. Leiden: E. J. Brill, 1993, p. 82.

Chinese Furniture Parts and Joinery

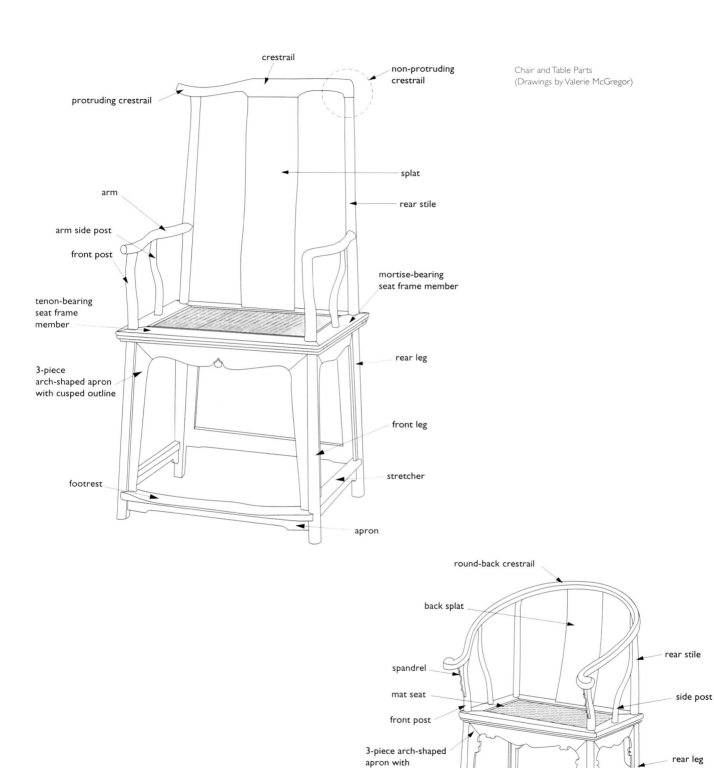

Chair and Table Parts
(Drawings by Valerie McGregor)

crestrail

non-protruding crestrail

protruding crestrail

splat

arm

rear stile

arm side post

front post

mortise-bearing seat frame member

tenon-bearing seat frame member

3-piece arch-shaped apron with cusped outline

rear leg

front leg

footrest

stretcher

apron

round-back crestrail

back splat

rear stile

spandrel

mat seat

side post

front post

3-piece arch-shaped apron with cusped outline

rear leg

front leg

stretcher

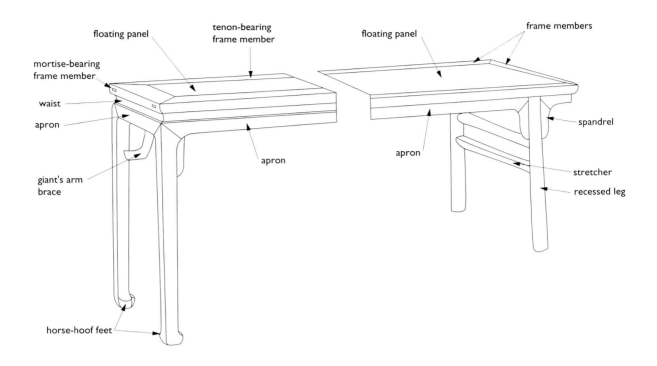

floating panel

tenon-bearing frame member

mortise-bearing frame member

waist

apron

giant's arm brace

horse-hoof feet

floating panel

frame members

apron

spandrel

stretcher

recessed leg

everted flange

apron

front leg

ornamental panel

rear leg

foot base

17

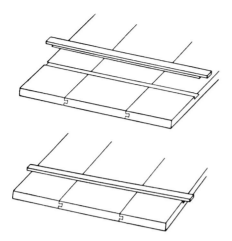

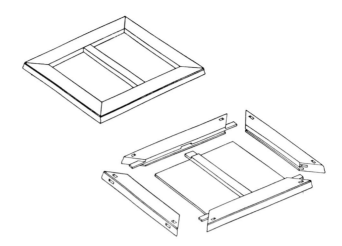

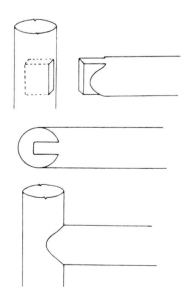

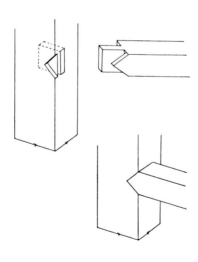

1. To join boards on a table top and to prevent their lifting up, a batten is slid through a sliding dovetail housing on the underside of the table.

2. On a seat frame or table top, the frame members are attached by a mitered mortise-and-tenon joint. A blind or exposed tenon on the frame member of the longer side fits into a mortise on the shorter frame member. Grooves on the inner edge of the framework accept the floating panel, and tenons on the tranverse brace fit into mortises on the front and back frame members.

3. When round-section stretchers join round legs on tables (see cat. 17) or arms join rear stiles of chairs (see cat. 8 and 10), a tenon with T-form enveloping sides on the end of the horizontal member fits into a corresponding mortise on the vertical member. This is called a frogmouth join.

4. Square-section stretchers are often joined to square-section legs on chairs (see cat. 7), and square-section rear stiles are often joined to square-section crestrails (see cat. 9), using the mitred, T-form mortise-and-tenon joint, with the extra front triangular projection fitting into a housing on the opposite member.

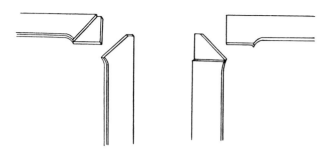

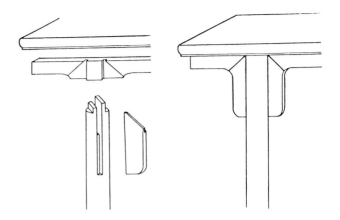

5. The pieces of a three-part framework between the legs of a chair (see cat. 8) are often joined by a half-lapped mitred join.

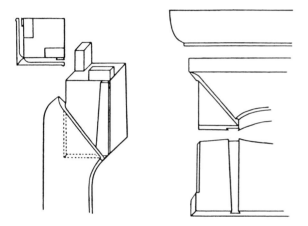

6. On a recessed-leg table (see cat. 17), the apron fits into a housing cut into the leg and the spandrels fit into grooves on the legs and into a mitered housing on the apron. Two long tenons on the top of the leg then fit into mortises on the underside of the tabletop.

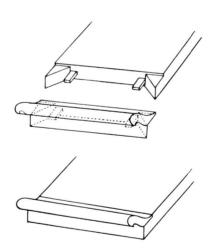

7. On a corner-leg waisted table (see cat. 20), the apron, with a tapered groove on its inner face, slips down over a tapered dovetail wedge on the leg. Two tenons located at the top of the leg then fit into mortises on the underside of the tabletop.

8. On a table with everted flanges (see cat. 19), two blind tenons on the tabletop fit into corresponding mortises on the everted flange and endboard.

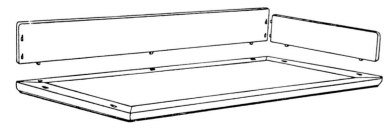

9. To join the rails of a couch-bed (see cat. 14 and 15), tapered tenons fit into mortises that are wider at one end, and then are slid downward and locked in place.

Drawings 1–9 are reproduced from Wang Shixiang, Connoisseurship of Chinese Furniture, published by Joint Publishing Co. (H.K.) Ltd., 1989. Courtesy of the publisher.

Xi Xiang Ji (Tale of the Western Chamber).
From Xiang Xue Ju edition, 1614.

Furnishing the Self in Early Modern China

Craig Clunas

> With the construction and furnishing of interior space from the fifteenth to the seventeenth century, Italians created a world in which they could develop a different style of life and in which a new culture came to be defined. Consumption was a creative force to construct a cultural identity. In inventing all kinds of new furnishings…Italians discovered new values and pleasures for themselves, reordered their lives with new standards of comportment, communicated something about themselves to others—in short generated culture, and in the process created identities for themselves. In this cultural development there was a dynamic for change that resulted from the interaction between people and physical objects.[1]

This passage by the modern American historian of the Italian Renaissance Richard Goldthwaite exemplifies an attitude toward the material things of the past that has engaged the attention of many scholars in recent years. It is based on the hypothesis that the relationship created between people and things is of central importance in the sustenance of social existence. It largely assumes that in the Europe of what is now often called the "early modern period," between about 1500 and 1800, that relationship underwent a decisive change, which in some sense explains the rise to global dominance of one particular civilization, known to itself as "the West."[2]

But there is a problem here. Stated quite simply, if we were to replace the word *Italians* with the word *Chinese* throughout, the passage above would still make perfect sense. In Ming-period China (1368–1644) too, consumption was "a creative force to construct a cultural identity." The Chinese empire's population in 1600 of about 150–175 million made it, by itself, equivalent in number of people to that supported by the entire space of western Europe. Its physical size was similar, too: it took a courier on horseback the same length of time to get from Beijing in the north to Canton in the south as it did to reach London from Venice. In China's great cities—no less than in Florence or Venice (both of which were medium-sized towns by Ming standards)—those who could afford to do so created identities for themselves through their use of things. In the sixteenth and seventeenth centuries, these were often new and different kinds of things, things necessary and things luxurious, locally made as well as imported from afar. Things that had only previously been available to a tiny minority came to be within the reach of a larger, if still small, proportion of the population—those not crushed by the stark necessity for survival. In the socially fluid and restless world of Ming China, where families and individuals could rise to fame and wealth and plunge into obscurity and poverty quite quickly, possessions gave rise to one of the types of social meaning that were deployed in the struggle for prominence and security.[3] Furniture was just one of the categories of goods so employed.

It was a category that was only at this period coming to be recognized as having a separate and distinct existence. Of course there had been furniture in China prior to the Ming period, and luxurious items of furniture certainly had been important to the elite for many centuries. But this is not the same as seeing

Xi Xiang Ji (Tale of the Western Chamber), 1640 edition.
Photo courtesy of Museum für Ostasiatische Kunst, Cologne.

it as a distinct and bounded group of objects in its own right. In the Ming period there was still no word for furniture that encompassed tables, chairs, beds, cupboards, and all the other forms seen in this exhibition. At that time, the word *jiaju*, which certainly means "furniture" in the modern Chinese language, meant something more like "household implements," and referred to a category that could still include domestic and agricultural tools.

In China in the sixteenth century, the concept of furniture as a category of object certainly existed, even before the use of a single word to describe it. When the functionaries of the state inventoried the property of the disgraced Grand Secretary Yan Song (1480–1565) in 1562, they did separate out certain types of objects, which we would now call pieces of furniture, as worthy of incorporation into the vast imperial storehouses. These were, however, objects of only two types, which were catalogued as follows:[4]

Screens and Folding Screens

Large standing screens with Dali-stone panels[5] (20)

Medium standing screens with Dali-stone panels (17)

Small standing screens with Dali-stone panels (19)

Standing screens with Lingbi-stone panels[6] (8)

Plain lacquered standing screens with white stone panels (5)

Standing screens with Qiyang-stone panels (5)

Large standing screen with panel of Japanese gold lacquer and colored painting (1)

Small standing screen with panel of Japanese gold lacquer and colored painting (1)

Large folding screens of Japanese gold lacquer with silver flakes (2)

Small folding screens of Japanese gold lacquer with silver flakes (3)

Folding screens of colored lacquer (4)

Folding screens with landscapes in painted gold (*miaojin*)[7] lacquer (3)

Folding screens of black lacquer with applied gold (*tiejin*) (2)

Large folding screens of painted sheepskin (2)

Medium folding screens of sheepskin (3)

Small folding screens of sheepskin (3)

Folding screens of Japanese gold lacquer painted with butterflies (5)

Folding screens of Japanese gold lacquer painted with flowers and grasses (2)

Folding screens with pine, prunus, and bamboo in "muddy gold" (*nijin*) (2)

Folding screens with landscapes in "muddy gold" (1)

A total of one hundred and eight standing and folding screens

Beds Inlaid with Dali Stone and Mother-of-Pearl, etc.[8]

Bed of carved lacquer with Dali-stone inlay (1)

Bed of black lacquer with Dali-stone inlay (1)

Bed of mother-of-pearl-inlaid lacquer with Dali-stone inlay (1)

Canopied bed⁹ of lacquer with Dali-stone inlay (1)
Bed in the shape of the character *shan* (mountain) with Dali-stone inlay (1)
Bed of modeled, mother-of-pearl-inlaid, and painted-gold lacquer (1)
Beds inlaid with mother-of-pearl with dressing chambers (3)
Canopied cool beds inlaid with mother-of-pearl (5)
Rattan beds with comb-shaped backs inlaid with mother-of-pearl (2)
Bed with folding screens edged in tortoise shell (1)
A total of seventeen beds

Several things are striking about this list. One perhaps surprising thing it shows is the presence of luxury objects imported from Japan in the Ming interior. Over 10 percent of Yan Song's screens were from Japan. Some of these may have been of painted paper, while some may have been decorated in the *maki-e,* or "sprinkled-picture," technique of lacquering on wood, which Chinese craftsmen of the sixteenth century could attempt to imitate but could not match. The notion of Ming China as a hermit society, isolated from and suspicious of the outside world, which is still sometimes repeated in textbooks, is simply not true. Those foreign goods that suited the lifestyles of the rich (and Japanese items were the most prominent among these), were eagerly adopted.

A second point to notice is the prominence of lacquered furniture, decorated in the variety of inlaying, carving, painting, and other techniques that perhaps reached their apogee in the Ming period and continued on into the succeeding Qing period (1644–1911). This may not be the image of Chinese furniture that immediately springs to mind today, when it is objects in wood alone that sit more comfortably with modernist aesthetic ideals. However, all the evidence points to the fact that the most valuable furniture of the Ming was lacquered. Its rate of survival is in inverse proportion to the esteem in which it was once held, and only very occasional pieces survive to give us some dim sense of the splendor of the furnishings of the mansion of someone like Yan Song in his prime.

Nevertheless, it is very unlikely that Yan Song did not also have wooden furniture, even if these pieces were not the most expensive or noteworthy. The frames of the standing screens inlaid with panels of Dali stone, the material of which is not mentioned, were probably constructed of wood (although we cannot know the exact timbers involved). Examples of this form do survive, although again in nothing like the numbers that must once have been manufactured. Much of the ordinary furniture of his numerous mansions may well have been of wood, too, but it was thought to be too insignificant to be inventoried piece by piece. Instead, we have only aggregate figures for its value, which reveal that beds or couches were still the most important category of object to be treated separately, and that within that category lacquered wooden objects were still in the predominant majority:

Beds of Mother-of-Pearl-Inlaid and Painted Lacquer Converted to Cash[10]

Large "eight-pace" beds[11] of mother-of-pearl-inlaid lacquer, carved lacquer, or painted lacquer (52 items at 15 ounces of silver each)

Carved beds inlaid with Dali stone (8 items at 8 ounces of silver each)

Medium-sized "eight-pace" beds of painted lacquer or carved lacquer (145 items at 4.3 ounces of silver each)

Medium-sized bed of elm wood carved with poems and paintings (1 item at 5 ounces of silver)

Cool beds of painted gold lacquer with rattan and carved flowers (130 items at 2.5 ounces of silver each)

Small cool beds with screens in the form of the character *shan* (mountain), or of a comb (138 items at 1.5 ounces of silver each)

Cool beds of plain lacquer and *huali* wood (40 items at 1 ounce of silver each)

Various old and new wooden beds of miscellaneous patterns (126 items at a total of 83.35 ounces of silver)

However, here we have the first unequivocal mention on the inventory of objects in wood, the two timbers mentioned being elm (*ju*) and *huali*. This latter is, of course, the focus of much interest on the part of collectors and museums today, the material from which many of the objects in this exhibition are constructed. It may well have featured in the vast, anonymous mass of objects that were simply listed as follows:

Tables, Chairs, Cupboards, and Other Items Converted to Cash[12]

Tables (3,051 items at 0.25 ounces of silver each)

Chairs (2,493 items at 0.2 ounces of silver each)

Cupboards (376 items at 0.18 ounces of silver each)

Stools and benches (803 items at 0.05 ounces of silver each)

Stands and shelves (366 items at 0.08 ounces of silver each)

Footstools (355 items at 0.02 ounces of silver each)

The quantities in the inventory are certainly impressive in themselves, but can this list, with its bland bureaucratic language, tell us anything at all about the attitudes of an owner (albeit an owner as unusual as Yan Song) in the Ming period concerning his possessions? Can we use it to discern anything at all about how this mass of material was used in the creation of a social identity? What are these things *for*, in anything other than the strictly utilitarian sense?

We might start by considering the question of beds or couches (*chuang*). Why are there so many of them, and why are they, alone of all the forms furniture can take, singled out for special treatment? How did Yan Song get them, and how did he use them? Many of them were clearly visually striking and impressive objects, but just who saw them; whom were they designed to impress?

One possible parallel with the situation in contemporary Europe can be disposed of immediately. A Ming grandee like Yan Song did not go to bed in public, there was no royal *coucher* as there was at the court of the French king Louis XIV, where privileged favorites would ceremonially help the monarch to disrobe and get into bed. The disposition of space in the Ming mansion meant that the sleeping space of neither women nor men of the upper classes was public space. Guests were not received there, as they were in the early modern European "chamber." Nor would etiquette have permitted a man like Yan Song to receive guests in a reclining position on a couch. For the ruling class, decorum, and the right to rule that went with it, was bound up in a body language of verticality, rigidity, and control. In fact, part of the attraction of drama, fiction, and the illustrated editions in which they were published, may have been derived from their abilities to reveal to the gaze of the spectator (usually the male spectator), the intimate living space of others. The illustrated books of the Ming period revealed the arena of a supposedly private self, not the public self presented in the more formal reception areas of the house. Here, a different set of furniture types prevailed.

Other explanations must therefore be sought to explain the prominence of lacquered beds and couches. One of these may lie in a gendered understanding of the bed as a social sign in Ming China, and in its particular importance to women. A woman's bed, along with her jewelry, was viewed in Ming China as a physical embodiment of her position within the household. It might form part of her dowry, provided at marriage by her family, and as such would be carried through the streets at her wedding, more visible to public scrutiny than the woman herself. Or it might be provided for her by her husband, as a mark of special esteem, in a polygamous social context where a number of women, as wives and concubines, each had her own living space and all the furnishings that went with it. This role of the bed is little documented in formal historical sources of the Ming period, but it comes through powerfully in one of the richest texts of world literature, the novel *Jin Ping Mei*, known in English variously as *The Golden Lotus* or *The Plum in the Golden Vase*.[13]

This vast, tightly constructed story, set in the household of the rich but thuggish Ximen Qing, is a cautionary tale of excess in the realms of emotions, passions, physical desires, and appetites; excess of luxurious living and conspicuous consumption. It is set in a world where money and brute force can procure anything. The novel, first published in about 1618, has a piquant connection with Yan Song and his family. A later romantic legend has it that the book (which is, in fact, anonymous) was written by the great scholar Wang Shizhen (1526–90) to revenge himself on Yan Shifan (1513–65), son of Yan Song and a man even more corrupt, greedy, and vicious than his father. The story goes that Yan Shifan had driven Wang's father to his death, and that in revenge Wang had written the (often highly erotic) *Jin Ping Mei* and presented it to his enemy. As the lascivious Yan licked his fingers in his haste to turn the pages, a poison impregnated in the paper slowly but surely carried him off to a horrible death.[14]

Legends aside, the *Jin Ping Mei* remains a rich source for many aspects of the material culture of the Ming period, furniture being one of them.[15] The novel reveals, for example, that a bride's trousseau might well include "beds and curtains, dressing case, chests, and cupboards of gold-painted lacquer."[16] It shows that a wife's ranking within the unstable pecking-order of the patriarchal household was reflected by the degree of lavishness of her lacquered bed, and these objects are described in the novel in exactly the same technical terms as are used in the Yan Song inventory. To underscore her supremacy over her rival, the newest wife, Pan Jinlian, demands and obtains from her husband a lavish chambered bed of lacquer inlaid with mother-of-pearl, which costs the huge sum of sixty ounces of silver.[17] (This price, perhaps, should not be taken literally, but rather as the novelist's indication of Ximen Qing's profligate ways with money.) This bed plays a role much later in the story, after Ximen Qing himself is dead, his family dispersed, its members reduced to poverty or deceased. One of Pan Jinlian's former maids visits the now derelict mansion and asks after the bed.

> "Where has our mistress's bed gone? Why has it vanished?" Xiaoyu said, "It went off with the Third Lady when she got married." …Chunmei heard this and lowered her head, tears prickling in her eyes. She said nothing but thought, "I remember how the mistress made a great fuss and wouldn't weaken, asking the master to buy her that bed. I really wanted to get that bed back, in remembrance of her. I never thought they would let someone have it." She couldn't help feeling a heartache as she asked Yueniang, "Then where is the Sixth Lady's mother-of-pearl-inlaid bed?" Yueniang said, "It's hard to explain…. I had no ready cash in the house so I had it taken away and sold." Chunmei asked, "How much did you sell it for?" Yueniang said, "Only thirty-five ounces of silver." Chunmei said, "What a shame! I heard the master say that bed was originally worth over sixty ounces. To sell it for so little! If I had known before that you were getting rid of it I would have given you thirty or forty ounces myself, I wanted it so much."[18]

The sale of the furniture and, above all, of the beds, represents the family's final degradation and bankruptcy. While, in the course of the sixteenth century, other kinds of luxury items and artwork were in the process of becoming full commodities, which were bought and sold freely and which sloughed off most of the associations with their previous owners once they had changed hands, furniture was perceived differently. It embodied the family's stability and coherence. It was sold only in extreme circumstances and such deacquisition was a clear disgrace.

We know little of the real Yan Song's private domestic life, since these are not the kinds of issues with which the historical sources of the day concern themselves. However it is likely that his household was home to more than one woman, and each of them would have had her own compound and her own servants. We can speculate that, as new furniture was acquired—perhaps more fashionable or more lavish furniture—older pieces would never have been disposed of, but might instead have been handed down to maids or other members of the household. They might be stored against the day when, in their turn, they would be needed as dowries, given to women of the household when they were given in marriage.

But how was such furniture acquired? Again *Jin Ping Mei* gives us a clue to at least one possibility. In chapter 45, an impoverished aristocratic family is forced to pawn with Ximen Qing a "standing screen of mother-of-pearl inlaid and gold-painted lacquer, with a Dali-stone panel."[19] This screen, described in exactly the same terms as those used in the inventory, must be a sizeable table screen, as it is further described as being three *chi* (the Ming foot of approximately 30 cm) wide and five *chi* high. It is accompanied by two lacquered gong stands. The pawning of these objects is probably not a straightforward commercial transaction. The family members ask only thirty ounces of silver for the three pieces, even though they are openly valued at fifty ounces. It is likely, therefore, that this is a disguised form of gift, a way of placing the givers under the protection of the increasingly powerful Ximen Qing and obliging him to come to their aid in future. Pawnbroking was a perfectly respectable and highly lucrative way of making money, and was engaged in by many high members of the Ming bureaucracy.

In the mid-sixteenth century, and until his fall from power, no one was more powerful than Yan Song, and no one's patronage was more avidly sought than his. He dominated the central imperial bureaucracy and, through it, networks of clients who stretched right across the empire. As such he was the recipient of immense quantities of gifts of all kinds. Ming China was a culture in which gifts and gift giving provided a crucial form of social cement among the elite. By modern standards many of these gifts were "bribes" and, indeed, at least some would have been categorized as such at the time if an official was unfortunate enough to fall from power. But the acceptance of gifts did not necessarily imply corruption in the eyes of people at the time. Gifts created relationships between people, and gave concrete form to relationships that already existed. Often these relationships were made visible through gifts, which did not need to be very costly or extraordinary objects. Indeed the most common gifts between members of the upper classes were small items of food, cakes or fruit, which were conveyed to their recipients in elaborately decorated lacquer boxes. The box was not retained by the recipient of the gift, but was returned, often containing a small return present destined as a tip for the servant who carried out the transaction. These food boxes (*shi he*) survive today in some numbers from the Ming period. One Ming text tells how the author once saw the street outside the headquarters of the military commandant of Nanjing, the southern capital, literally blocked by the food boxes presented to this grandee by the prominent families of the city.[20]

These gifts were *publicly* visible, manifesting to all who cared to look the existence of a relationship between the giver and the recipient. In this respect, they were rather like the large ceremonial gifts of flowers that are given today in China, and by Chinese people worldwide, to mark the opening of a new business venture or to celebrate some other major life event. It is arguable that, in the

Ming period, the very material of lacquer carried associations of the gift, and of ceremonial rather than utilitarian exchanges. It was, for example, used for a very special type of box, in which horoscopes of the bride and groom were exchanged at weddings.[21] Going one stage further, it is possible to speculate that at least some of the lavish and luxurious pieces of lacquer furniture in the possession of Yan Song, particularly the screens, had come to him as presents. From an analysis of the specifically auspicious subject matter on many pictures, we certainly know that a large proportion of his painting collection consisted of what came to be known as "gift paintings."[22] All cultures single out certain kinds of objects especially appropriate for gifts in particular situations. Often babies are given clothes but adults rarely are, while in Britain clocks and watches are traditional retirement presents. Given the role of lacquer in Ming gift culture, it is highly likely that at least some of Yan Song's lacquer screens and couches came to him in this way. The scale of a piece of furniture was important here. Carried through the streets prior to presentation, pieces of furniture given as gifts were a very public way of letting anyone who cared to look know that the giver and Yan Song were connected by the unequal but powerful relationship of protection sought and granted, gifts offered and accepted.

Furniture had another advantage in this respect. It was not a specific focus of the sumptuary laws by which the Ming state sought to regulate the consumption of luxuries, forcing each stratum of society to use only those types of dress, furniture, and utensils that were deemed appropriate to it.[23] In laws passed in 1393, and hardly updated in the course of the period, officials were forbidden to have beds or couches decorated with a design of five-clawed dragons, or of red lacquer decorated with gold. This left immense scope for the deployment of the many other lavish techniques of decoration that the Ming lacquerer had at hand. To the framers of the law, textiles and dress, not furniture, were the major focus of anxiety about inappropriate consumption. Although the laws seem to have been widely flouted, they could still be invoked when a high official fell from favor and was then discovered to possess robes decorated with forbidden patterns theoretically restricted to the imperial family. This could be the final nail in the coffin. After his arrest, Yan Song's furniture might have been further testimony to his lavishness—and hence probably to his greed and corruption—but it would never have been the thing that got him into trouble in the first place.

Although they were buried within the depths of his numerous mansions, it is possible that Yan Song's lacquer beds and lacquer screens, the most important pieces of furniture he possessed, were in a sense *public* objects. At a key moment in their biographies as objects, they might have been *seen* in all their splendor, carried through the streets on the backs of porters, laid down at the gates of mansions in busy streets in cities like Beijing and Nanchang, where he had his dwellings. They related to his public persona as an official, a man of wealth and power. Rather than saying anything about his personality, they told people who he was in the sense of what he could do. They manifest one kind of relationship between people and things, a relationship in which one type of self is constructed out of rank and position, with goods appropriate to that rank being fixed and stable. This is the kind of relationship between people and things that the sumptuary laws sought to pin firmly in place.

They were, however, never likely to succeed. In the course of the sixteenth century in China, other types of engagement between people and objects arose to contest this ideal, immobile world. To a large extent they were the inevitable product of commercial prosperity and economic growth, and of the resultant social fluidity they brought in their wake. This worried many people. After about 1520 the number of complaints about luxury and excess in the consumption of goods grew ever greater. These concentrated again on the issue of dress, the most obvious and yet troubling way in which social roles could be blurred: "Nowadays men dress in brocaded and embroidered silks, and women ornament themselves with gold and pearls, in a case of boundless extravagance which flouts the regulations of the state."[24]

Furniture inevitably was part of this discourse concerning luxury and excess. It is in this context that a writer named Fan Lian (b. 1540) recorded one of the key observations that, since it was brought to light in 1985 by the modern doyen of Chinese furniture studies, Wang Shixiang, has helped shape our understanding of hardwood, as opposed to lacquered, furniture. Of the years after 1567 Fan recalls:

> At that time, the wealthy families did not consider *ju* wood good enough and so it had become customary for them to have all their beds, cabinets, and tables made from *huali* wood, burl wood, blackwood, *xiangsi* wood [*jichi* wood], and boxwood. This furniture is very fine and exorbitant, each piece costing 10,000 cash, a most extravagant custom. It is strange that even those policemen who had a home would arrange a comfortable place to rest, separated by wooden partitions. In the courtyard they raised goldfish and planted various kinds of flowers. Inside there were good-quality wooden tables and a horsetail whisk for dusting. They called it the study. However, I really do not know what books they studied![25]

This is a relationship to objects in which things do not merely confirm the status that the person already holds, but can actually *change* that status. The presence of a fine table and a horsetail whisk can turn the side room of a house into the "study," and with it can transform their owner from a policeman into a "scholar." The apogee of this process is reached once again in the novel *Jin Ping Mei*, whose illiterate central character nevertheless still has his study (*shufang*) crammed with books bought by the yard, which he cannot read, and hung with supposed artistic masterpieces he is too crass to realize should not be hung in such promiscuous juxtapositions to each other.[26]

The vibrant commercial environment of Ming China's great cities was one in which any form of cultural service or culturally charged artifact could be bought for money. Paintings ancient and modern, antiques both real and forged, food and clothes and sexual gratification of all kinds, religious consolation, and geographical mobility were all available to those who could pay. Those of some means but of modest educations, who were not sure what to pay *for*, could first buy books that gave guidance on how to consume appropriately. These householder's manuals gave advice on a wide variety of practical and cultural topics, from how to make soya sauce at home to how to replicate a satisfyingly antique patina on a modern bronze vessel.[27] One illustrated example even helpfully includes a woodblock-printed picture of what a painting looks like, in case you have never seen one before. Indeed, the presence of pictures in books, now in much greater numbers and of much higher quality than at any previous period, fed the creation of a culture of visuality in which looking took on a new importance. There was more to look at, and more people were doing the looking.

A changed relationship to goods, which arguably came into play in China between about 1500 and 1600, took place at the same time as changes to certain conceptions of the self and of personal identity. These are expressed in philosophical writing and in imaginative literature, poetry in particular.[28] Whether, and how, the two types of change interrelate and interpenetrate each other is a complex question that remains to be solved. All the same, it is perhaps worth trying to map out some of the lines of inquiry that might be pursued.

When the revered literary figure Grand Secretary Li Dongyang (1447–1516) died, he, in his will, "divided the robes, court tablets, belts, inkstones, calligraphy, and paintings that he had used in his lifetime among his disciples." The author who recorded this fact went on to remark: "In all the writings that record the prime ministers of antiquity, there is nothing like this."[29] The point of the anecdote—its singularity, which makes it worthy of record—is that Li's property might normally have been expected to remain within his family, going entirely to his adopted son. Ming practice decreed that property was to be divided in strictly equal shares between all the male heirs. The son presumably did receive the bulk of the property, the family mansion and its furnishings, and the land that supported an elite lifestyle. The sharing out of personal items (none more personal than robes and belts) among men to whom he was related by ties of discipleship, suggests a degree of identification of the individual personality with the things. They are to act as secular relics, surviving tokens of the master-pupil relationship.

Visitors to a shrine to Li Dongyang, which was erected sometime after 1565, could see the actual tiny shoes and coat that he had worn when he was presented to the emperor as a child prodigy in 1450.[30] Here the object contains something of the person as an individual, not just as a grand secretary. This interest in relics of the great went along with a growing interest in gossip and anecdotes about prominent political or cultural figures, a type of writing that fills the literary genre known as *biji*, or "note-form" literature. These collections of brief anecdotal entries delight in telling us what people looked like, what they wore, how they spoke, even what they usually had for lunch, in a manner that suggests the existence of a remarkably modern interest in personality and celebrity by at least some Ming readers.

One related phenomenon of the later sixteenth century is the rise of the celebrity craftsmen or craftswomen—named makers of what had hitherto been anonymous, even if luxurious, craft products. It was in this century that the potters of Yixing started to sign the red stoneware teapots for which they were famous on an empirewide scale, and also from this century that the first reliable name of a jadecarver—Lu Zigang of Suzhou—comes down to us. Lu and a number of his contemporaries who became known for their mastery of other crafts were acceptable as dining partners to their ostensible social superiors, a fact that was recorded with astonishment by contemporaries. Their names alone—names like that of the metalworker Hu Wenming or the embroideress Han Ximeng—could multiply the price of an object many times, again to the amazement of writers at the time.[31] They may in reality have been "trademarks," guarantees of workshop quality rather than individual personalities, but the symbolic interest on the part of customers in having a name to deal with as a mark of excellence or reliability is striking all the same.

Could such personal identification take place in the case of furniture? Certainly we have at present only a single name out of all the furniture makers in Ming-period China (see cat. 18, note 3), which suggests that furniture stood lower in the hierarchy of the crafts than did some other types of objects. However we do not have the name of a single tailor either and, as we have seen in the case of Li Dongyang's robes, clothing could certainly be very powerfully associated with an individual owner.

At least one piece of evidence indicates that there was some space for a type of relationship of personal association between an owner and a piece of furniture in sixteenth-century China. It comes in relation not to a bed or a screen, but to two tables that played a role in the distinguished career of the official Gui Youguang (1507–71). In the section of his collected works entitled "Ming song zan" (Inscriptions, Rhapsodies, and Eulogies) are two very short pieces in the inscription form entitled, "Inscription on a Table" and "Inscription on a Table at Shunde Prefecture."[32] The objects themselves do not survive, of course, and we cannot be sure that we are dealing with words physically inscribed into a wooden or lacquered surface. (It does not seem impossible, however, that they were. See discussion for cat. 17). The first one is dated 1557, and speaks simply in thirty-five characters of the delights of studying the classics and histories, a discipline to which the author's whole heart is given in age no less than in his childhood. The table is not mentioned, but it is celebrated here as the specific and highly personal site of the intellectual endeavors that Gui Youguang sees as the central project of his life. The second inscription is longer and more circumstantial. It tells of how, when the author was nominally in charge of horse administration at a place called Xingzhou (he held this post from 1568), he in fact had no work to do, and no table on which he could pursue his beloved studies. When a storm knocked down many trees in the area, including innumerable willows, he obtained one of these, from which he had a table made. He then laments his uselessness in his present, minor post.

In no way can these inscriptions be construed as being about furniture or attitudes to furniture. All the same, they can suggest to us, if obliquely, some of the ways in which possessions and identities were mutually constructed by males of the upper classes (the only people whose explicit views have been recorded). For example, the central role of the table as the "site of the self" for men, paralleling the role of the bed for women, certainly deserves exploration in the future. It cannot be coincidental that a high proportion of the few dated or inscribed pieces of Ming or Qing furniture that have come down to us today are, in fact, tables of the kind generally used for writing or painting. It is highly likely that further trawls through the collected works of Ming writers would bring to light more such hints, from which a fuller picture could begin to emerge.

The writer He Liangjun (1506–73) was a close personal friend of the famous Suzhou poet, prose stylist, and painter Wen Zhengming (1470–1559), and he recorded many details of the great man's life, some solemn and some gossipy and personal. When he tried to characterize the greatness of the older man's renowned prose style, the natural simile that came to his mind compared literary effort to that required to bring out the grain in wood.[33] The word that linked the two ideas was *wen,* which originally meant something like "manifest pattern" or "markings," but which, by the Ming, had come to encompass an array of much more complex notions, including "literature" and "culture" itself.[34] The hardwood that was becoming fashionable as a furniture material at the very time when He Liangjun was writing was a visible manifestation of natural *wen* (sometimes called *"wen mu,"* patterned wood) and, although the idea is scarcely explicit in texts of the period, it may not be too far-fetched to accord it a metaphorical role in the minds of at least some who owned objects made out of it. Much more work needs to be done concerning the ways in which rough and smooth surfaces, reflecting and dull materials, were understood in the minds of Ming men and women before we can say any more about this intriguing possibility.

When the young, upper class writer Wen Zhenheng (1585–1645), the great-grandson of Wen Zhengming, wrote his *Zhang Wu Zhi* (Treatise on Superfluous Things), sometime between about 1610 and 1620, he entitled one of his twelve chapters "Tables and Couches."[35] A further chapter is devoted to placing and arrangement, or what we might call interior decorating. In both these chapters, furniture is integrated into a complete panorama of the luxury lifestyle, but it has an independent existence as one of the key components of that lifestyle, alongside and on a par with clothing, food, modes of transport, and what we would now call architecture. All of these categories, and his book as a whole, imply the existence of an ideal reader and consumer for his text—an autonomous male subject whose task in life is to discriminate between the "elegant" and the "vulgar," eschewing anything that, by its style, material, or decoration is redolent of those who by class or by gender are not fit to judge and hence not fit to rule. It is surely significant that the title of his chapter refers to tables and couches, using for the latter the word *ta,* and not *chuang,* thus signaling that he is talking about things for *men.*

It may be premature to see Wen's categories as being exactly the same as our modern ones, however. The very notion of the self with which he operates may differ from the concept that his French contemporary René Descartes (1596–1650) was in the process of constructing as normative in western Europe. Instead of a single "self" opposed to the world "out there," recent studies of the idea of the subject in China have emphasized the notion of a multiplicity of subject positions (as son, as father, as official, as recluse, as painter, as householder) that might be occupied at different moments.[36] By the late Ming period, notions of possession, property, and appropriate consumption had to negotiate with this multiplicity, perhaps providing the idea of fitting different things to different subject positions. Our understanding of the solid, tangible, wooden survivals of the Ming period, in the form of the furniture that has survived to be exhibited in museums and inserted into our frameworks of meaning, may yet prove to be more elusive—more hard to grasp than it appears at a first, admiring glance.

Notes

1. Richard A. Goldthwaite, *Wealth and the Demand for Art in Italy 1300–1600*. Baltimore and London, Johns Hopkins University Press, 1993, p. 243.

2. Other major works of scholarship to foreground the issue of consumption include: Neil McKendrick, John Brewer, and J.H. Plumb, *The Birth of a Consumer Society: The Commercialization of Eighteenth-Century England* (London: Europa, 1982); Chandra Mukerji, *From Graven Images: Patterns of Modern Materialism* (New York: Columbia University Press, 1983); Simon Schama, *The Embarrassment of Riches: An Interpretation of Dutch Culture in the Golden Age* (London: Collins, 1987).

3. This forms the theme of Craig Clunas, *Superfluous Things: Material Culture and Social Status in Early Modern China* (Cambridge and Chicago: Polity Press, 1991).

4. *Tian shui bing shan lu*, (A Record of the Waters of Heaven Melting the Iceberg), in *Wuzong wai ji*, Zhongguo lishi yanjiu ziliao congshu. Shanghai: Shanghai Shudian, 1982, pp. 128–29.

5. Dali stone, named after the town of Dali in Yunnan province, is a striated marble. See Wen Zhenheng, *Zhang wu zhi jiao zhu*, (Annotated "Treatise on Superfluous Things." Nanjing: Jiangsu kexue jishu chubanshe, 1984, p. 117).

6. Lingbi stone was named after Lingbi county in Anhui province; it was among the most prized stones in the Ming.

7. *Miaojin, tiejin,* and *nijin* were different qualities of gold-decorated lacquer. For these techniques and the differences between them, see Wang Shixiang *Xiushilu jieshuo*, (An Explanation of "Records of Lacquering") (Beijing: Wenwu chubanshe, 1983, p. 78).

8. A slight problem of terminology exists here. The Chinese word *chuang* in Ming sources can be interpreted to mean both the types of furniture now translated into English as "bed" (which usually means canopied bed), and *couch* or *daybed*. I have chosen not to differentiate and have always translated *chuang* as "bed."

9. The names for different kinds of beds referred to the presence or absence of a canopy and a solid or textile surround. See Craig Clunas, *Chinese Furniture*, Victoria and Albert Museum Far Eastern Series (London: Bamboo Books, 1988, p. 31).

10. *Tian shui bing shan lu*, pp. 159–60.

11. The eight-pace bed (*ba bu chuang*) was the largest type. It had solid sides and an integral antechamber. Clunas, *Chinese Furniture*, p. 31.

12. *Tian shui bing shan lu*, p. 162.

13. The first volume of the definitive translation into English, by David Todd Roy, has appeared as *The Plum in the Golden Vase, or Chin P'ing Mei*, vol. 1: *The Gathering*. (Princeton Library of Asian Translations. Princeton, N.J.: Princeton University Press, 1993). This replaces all older translations, such as Clement Egerton, *The Golden Lotus*, 4 vols. (London: Routledge & Kegan Paul, 1939; reprinted 1972). The best existing translation in a European language is André Lévy, *Fleur en fiole d'or*, 2 vols. (Paris: Gallimard, 1985). References to the Chinese text below are to *Jin Ping Mei cihua*, 4 vols. (Taibei: Zengnizhi wenhua shiye gongsi, 1980–81).

14. Lévy, pp. 51-52.

15. Craig Clunas, "The Novel *Jin Ping Mei* as a Source for the Study of Ming Furniture," *Orientations* 23.1 (January 1992), pp. 60–68, attempts to list some of the most useful passages. See also Curtis Evarts, "The Novel *Jin Ping Mei*: A Comparison of Seventeenth- and Eighteenth-Century Illustrations," *Journal of the Classical Furniture Society* 3.4 (Autumn 1993), pp. 21–45.

16. *Jin Ping Mei cihua*, III, p. 461. The bed is also the central part of the dowry of Ximen Qing's daughter and of his third wife, Meng Yulou, when she remarries after his death. Idem., III, p. 372.

17. *Jin Ping Mei cihua*, I, p. 435.

18. *Jin Ping Mei cihua*, III, p. 442. More full translation in Clunas, "The Novel *Jin Ping Mei*," pp. 67–68.

19. *Jin Ping Mei cihua*, II, p. 155.

20. He Liangjun, *Si you zhai cong shuo*, Yuan Ming shiliao biji congkan. Beijing: Zhonghua shuju, 1983, p. 103.

21 Craig Clunas, "Books and Things: Ming Literary Culture and Material Culture," in Frances Wood, ed., *Chinese Studies*, British Library Occasional Papers 10. London: British Library, 1988, pp. 136–43.

22. Guo Licheng, "Zengli hua yanjiu" (A Study on Gift Paintings), in *International Colloquium on Chinese Art History, 1991: Proceedings. Painting and Calligraphy*, Part 2. Taipei: National Palace Museum, 1992, pp. 749–66.

23. Clunas, *Superfluous Things*, pp. 147–52, and Craig Clunas, "Regulation of Consumption and the Institution of Correct Morality by the Ming State," in Chün-chieh Huang and Erik Zürcher, eds., *Norms and the State in China*, Sinica Leidensia 28. Leiden, New York, Cologne: Brill, 1993, pp. 39–49.

24. Zhang Han, *Song chuang meng yu* (1593), quoted in Clunas, "Regulation of Consumption," pp. 45–46.

25. Quoted in Wang Shixiang, *Classic Chinese Furniture: Ming and Early Qing Dynasties*, translated by Sarah Handler and the author. London: Han-Shan Tang, 1986, p. 14.

26. *Jin Ping Mei cihua*, I, p. 496.

27. Clunas, *Superfluous Things*, pp. 37–38.

28. Wm. Theodore de Bary, "Individualism and Humanitarianism in Late Ming Thought," in Wm. Theodore de Bary, ed., *Self and Society in Ming Thought*. New York: Columbia University Press, 1970, pp. 145–248.

29. He Liangjun, p. 67.

30. L. Carrington Goodrich and Chaoying Fang, eds., *Dictionary of Ming Biography*, 2 vols. New York and London: Columbia University Press, 1976, p. 879.

31. Clunas, *Superfluous Things*, pp. 61–64.

32 Gui Youguang, *Zhenchuan xiansheng ji* (Collected Works of Master Zhenchuan), 2 vols., Zhongguo gudian wenxue congshu. Shanghai: Shanghai guji chubanshe, 1981, p. 652.

33. He Liangjun, p. 212.

34. Peter K. Bol, *"This Culture of Ours": Intellectual Transitions in T'ang and Sung China*. Stanford: Stanford University Press, 1992, p. 85.

35. Wen Zhenheng, pp. 225–45.

36. This idea is central to the essays in Angela Zito and Tani E. Barlow, eds., *Body, Subject and Power in China* (Chicago: Chicago University Press, 1994).

Wood Shaped and Standing through the Winds of Time: The Evolution of Chinese Furniture

Sarah Handler

The furniture in this exhibition represents the culmination of a long tradition, a historical plateau when the finest materials, design, and construction were harmoniously combined. That these pieces have survived is largely due to the fact that, except for the lacquered ones, they are fashioned from long-lasting hardwoods. In China, the extensive use of hardwoods for furniture began only in the mid-sixteenth century. Prior to that time most pieces were fashioned from less-durable softwoods. Hardwood construction permits a slender austerity of furniture design, which is one of its appealing characteristics.

The furniture of this period belongs to a time when China was the only Asian nation to have adopted the chair-level mode of living. In about the tenth century it had become common in China to sit on elevated seats at high tables (fig. 3). Previously people sat on mats or low platforms and used low tables and armrests—the mat-level mode of living (fig. 4). With the advent of the chair-level mode of living, furniture became elevated and a more important component of the interior. By the seventeenth century many new types and forms had developed, as had resultant innovations in design and construction. But nonetheless, the new furniture was the product of a long evolution, with features that can be traced back to very early times. The astonishing persistence of ancient elements, transformed into new creations, contributed decisively to the art of Chinese furniture.

Tables

Tables comprise the most prevalent type of furniture in mat-level China and the earliest extant examples predict forms that would be produced some three thousand years later. A small bronze table used for food offerings to the ancestors, from the Anyang period (thirteenth–eleventh century B.C.) of the Shang found in a storage pit in Hua'erlou, Yi Xian, Liaoning province, is probably similar in design to simpler wooden tables used at banquets for the living (fig. 1). The legs of this early table slant slightly inward toward the top in a construction derived from wooden architecture and characteristic of later armchairs with protruding crestrails and tapered cabinets (cat. 8, 26, and 27).

The arched and cusped opening between the legs of the Shang table is a feature commonly found, often with decorative elaborations, on hardwood chairs and couch-beds (cat. 8 and 15). The rim around the top of the bronze table later evolved into the water-stopping molding (cat. 22). Each side of the base of the offering table is embellished with a large *taotie* (stylized animal face). The *taotie* is composed of motifs arranged in reversed symmetry on either side of a central axis, a design principle that dominates early bronze decor as well as the carvings ornamenting hardwood furniture. On the aprons of hardwood tables and seats, running dragons frequently face each other on either side of a central motif (cat. 15). Reversed symmetry also prevails in more abstract ornamentation, such as that on the aprons flanking the legs of the long side table (cat. 19).

Fig. 1. Small sacrificial table. Found at Hua'erlou, Yi Xian, Liaoning. Anyang period of the Shang (thirteenth–eleventh century B.C.). Bronze; height 14.3 cm, width 33.6 cm, depth 17.7 cm. Liaoning Provincial Museum.

(Liaoning Sheng Bowuguan (Liaoning Provincial Museum). *Zhongguo bowuguan congshu di san juan. Liaoning Sheng Bowuguan* (The Museums of China, vol. 3, Liaoning Provincial Museum). Beijing: Wenwu Press, 1983, p. 16)

Fig. 2. Small sacrificial table. Found in tomb no. 4, Zhaoxiang, Dangyang, Hubei. Spring and Autumn Period (770–475 B.C.). Lacquered wood; height 14.5 cm, width 24.5 cm, depth 19 cm.

(After Yichang Area Museum (Excavation of Tomb No. 4 of the Spring and Autumn Period at Zhaoxiang in Dangyang, Hubei). *Wenwu* 1990.10 (M4:13), pl. 1)

Fig. 3. Detail of twelfth-century copy of painting attributed to Gu Hongzhong. *The Night Revels of Han Xizai,* Five Dynasties period, tenth century. Handscroll, ink and colors on silk; height 29 cm, width 338.3 cm. Palace Museum, Beijing.

(Photo courtesy of Wango Weng)

The construction of wooden furniture evolved from ancient wooden architecture. For instance, the column, beam, and strut architectural framework led to the stretcher-and-struts form of construction used to strengthen later tables, daybeds, and chairs (cat. 17, 13, and 7). This is seen as early as the tenth century B.C. on a tablelike stand attached to the ritual bronze vessel known as *Ling gui* (Musée Guimet, Paris), on which the legs are connected by a high, horizontal bar with short verticals attaching it to the top.[1] The bronze stand of the *Ling gui,* like the Shang offering table, is undoubtedly modeled after a wooden prototype.

The earliest extant wooden furniture was found in Eastern Zhou (770–221 B.C.) tombs. By this time some of the constructions basic to later furniture were already in use, among them mitered, mortised-and-tenoned frames; exposed and hidden tenons; dovetailed tenons; double-dovetailed loose tenons; exposed-corner dovetails;[2] and the tenon and plug joint used on "giant's arm braces"[3] (cat. 20 and 9).

A small, lacquered, wooden sacrificial table (*zu*) from the southern state of Chu was discovered in a Spring and Autumn period (770–475 B.C.) tomb at Zhaoxiang in Dangyang, Hubei (fig. 2). The table is strikingly similar to later pieces and has rectangular spandrels that foreshadow those commonly found on furniture (cat. 17 and 18) since the Song period (960–1279) (fig. 3). Spandrels and legs are attached to the tabletop with simple mortise-and-tenon joins. Clearly the strongly upturned ends of the top are predecessors of later everted flanges (cat. 19). The top of the table is red lacquer and the sides and legs have a black-lacquer background covered with vigorous red-lacquer paintings of imaginary creatures that undoubtedly had a potent magical significance. By the seventeenth century the techniques of lacquer painting had become very sophisticated and the elaborate floral designs purely decorative (cat. 18 and 24). Depictions of ritual observances engraved on Eastern Zhou bronze vessels show wine jars on tables

Fig. 4. Stone engraving from the tomb at Anqiu, Shandong, second century A.D. Ink rubbing.

(After Liao Ben. "Zhongguo zaoqi yan juchang suo shu-lue" (Performing Sites of China's Earlier Period). *Wenwu* 1990.4, p. 63)

with upturned ends. Some of these ancient tables are high, suggesting that even in mat-level times furniture was occasionally elevated.[4]

The upturned ends give the Zhaoxiang sacrificial table a monumentality different in spirit from the low, rectangular, lacquered-wood tray-tables (*an*) used for serving food that were found in the tomb of a fourth-century B.C. Chu ruler at Xinyang in Henan. One of the most elegant of these tray-tables is beautifully painted with a rondel pattern and has bronze, hoof-shaped legs, bronze corner-mounts, and bronze rings suspended from stylized animal faces.[5] Here, as in later furniture, bronze is used both decoratively and functionally. Other tray-tables have two or three legs on each side tenoning into side stretchers, a form that later evolved into carved panels above the foot base (cat. 19).

Fig. 5. Eight-lobed offering stand, eighth century. Wood painted white with green, gold, and silver decoration; height 10.2 cm, diameter 44.7 cm. Shoso-in, Nara, Japan.

(After *Treasures of the Shosoin*. Shosoin Office, ed. Tokyo: Asahi Shimbun, 1965, plate 71)

Sacrificial tables (smaller and slightly higher than the tray-tables) and armrests were also found in the Xinyang tombs. The armrests are fashioned from carved or painted lacquered wood, and one luxurious model is inlaid with white jade,[6] foreshadowing the more refined mother-of-pearl inlay on the armchairs in catalogue number 10.

Low tables continued to be popular in the Han period (206 B.C.–220 A.D.) and now we find a new form: low tables with a number of curved legs tenoning into side stretchers. These curved-leg tables came in a variety of sizes, according to their function. Long ones were used in front of low platforms for serving food and drink at a grand banquet, and both long and short models functioned as desks and chopping boards in the kitchen. Round stands supported pots of wine; the wine was ladled into cups, which were placed on round trays and carried to the long tables. Small, individual, rectangular dining tables were also placed on the floor in front of seating mats and platforms (fig. 4). The legs of these tables were straight or modeled like the legs of a hoofed animal, and were frequently made of metal. When not in use, the small tables were stacked in the kitchen.

There were also small square tables used for *liubo,* a game of divination. An exceptionally fine one was found in a Western Han (206 B.C.–24 A.D.) tomb in

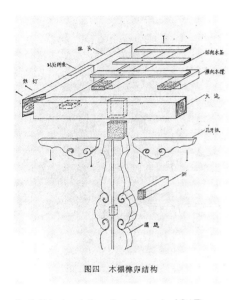

图四 木棚榫卯结构

Fig. 6a. Wooden platform, from the tomb of Cai Zhuang, Qianjiang, Jiangsu. Five Dynasties, 927–929. Height 57 cm, width 188 cm, depth 94 cm. Yangzhou Museum.

Fig. 6b. Sketch depicting mortise-and-tenon joinery of wooden platform above.

(Chen Zengbi. "Qian nian guta" (A Thousand-Year-Old Ta). *Wenwu*, 1984.6, pp. 66 and 67)

Sanjiaowei, Tianchang county, Anhui.[7] It is black lacquer with red delineating board markings and exquisite decorations of clouds and kneeling men. At opposite sides of the table are two drawers in which were found eighteen game pieces. The table is thus an early, mat-level version of the high, hardwood game tables with drawers and removable tops concealing multiple game boards. Moreover, it is a predecessor of the square dining table (cat. 21) that, after the meal, might be used for playing games on a separate hardwood board.

Low game tables were used in the Tang period (618–906), and by its end high, square tables had come to be employed for food preparation. A painting in cave eighty-five at Dunhuang shows a butcher at work. In this image are two large, square tables with recessed, splayed legs, serving as chopping boards.[8] The Tang period is the transitional period between the mat-level and chair-level modes of living. Low furniture was in fashion, such as the elegant tables and stands found in the Shoso-in in Japan. The pieces were imported from China or made after Chinese models. The stands, used for incense and other offerings to Buddha, have cabriole legs in imaginative variations of leaf forms, delicately painted in gold, silver, and other colors (fig. 5). In later periods, small stands, which were placed on high tables to elevate precious objects, sometimes displayed comparatively whimsical designs that contrast with the austerity of larger pieces. Incense burners, fantastic rocks, and vases of flowers were raised up on high, free-standing stands. Often these stands are round with five legs resting on a continuous base stretcher (cat. 23). Lacquer examples are more ornate in shape and decoration, as in the model with cabriole legs shown in catalogue number 24. The graceful lines of this stand are the culmination of the long evolution of the cabriole leg, which traces its origins to Shang bronzes.

During the Tang period, people began to eat while seated on long benches or stools around large, low, rectangular tables. A wall painting found in a tomb in Nanliwang, Changan county, Shaanxi, shows feasters seated cross-legged or with their legs pendant on benches that are almost the same height as the table. Like the table, these benches have four recessed legs.[9] This uncomfortable relationship between the height of table and seat is characteristic of the transitional period.

By the Song, tables as well as seats had come to be elevated so that diners could sit comfortably around a table and help themselves from dishes placed in the center. Dining customs were now very different from when people had their own individual table and didn't serve themselves from communal dishes. Furniture was no longer a prerogative of the elite, and Song paintings show that in even the humblest wineshops ordinary people sat raised up on benches around high tables. Once furniture was elevated it became a more important component of the interior and new types and forms developed. The domestic interior changed radically, its spaces were divided into rooms, its ceilings became higher, its windows were raised above floor level, and hanging scrolls decorated the walls.

An early depiction of the new chair-level mode of living appears in a handscroll generally considered to be a twelfth-century copy of *The Night Revels of Han Xizai* (Palace Museum, Beijing), a painting attributed to the tenth-century painter Gu Hongzhong (fig. 3). Han Xizai was an accomplished and learned gentleman who deliberately led a dissipated existence to avoid being appointed to an official government post. The emperor was suspicious, however, and wanted to discover if there was any truth in the stories about Han's lavish and licentious parties. So he sent Gu Hongzhong to attend one of the banquets and paint what he saw—and what he saw was most improper by Confucian standards.

Sporting a beard and tall hat, Han is shown seated, his legs up on a couch, with a red-robed friend. A low table with refreshments, only partially visible, stands on the couch between them. Here the old mat-level mode of living has been elevated to chair-level height and exists side-by-side with high tables and chairs. Small, low tables such as this one were used, too, on beds and *kangs*—the high, built-in, heated platforms of northern China. They are one of the common types of later tables (cat. 25). In the painting, wine and food are also placed on two rectangular tables in front of the couch. These high tables have round, recessed legs, side stretchers, and simple curvilinear spandrels that evolved from the spandrels on the Zhaoxiang sacrificial table (fig. 2). This shape, with slight variations, has been found in an actual table as well as tomb models and tomb paintings from the eleventh and twelfth centuries, and it has remained popular ever since (cat. 17 and 18). It is so ubiquitous that it can be called the "standard table." The tables depicted in *The Night Revels of Han Xizai* are still not quite high enough to enable the gentleman seated in front of the screen to fit his legs underneath.

High square tables came into common use for dining during the Song. In Zhang Zeduan's early twelfth-century painting *Spring Festival on the River* (Palace Museum, Beijing), we see them in both fancy restaurants and simple eateries. They were also used for preparing and serving food, wine, and tea. An elegant one for serving tea is depicted in the tomb of the Daoist Feng Daozhen (d. c. 1265) at Datong, Shanxi.[10] It has corner legs, stretchers on all sides, and beading outlining the sides of the top. The legs end in cloud-head feet, a common Song termination also found on the couch-bed in figure 6. Square tables for eating could not interfere with the legs of a seated diner and had to be sturdy. Thus, by the Ming period (1368–1644) a form had evolved with humpback stretchers, and an inset panel between the top and apron that is known as a "waist," a construction adopted from earlier Buddhist pedestals (cat. 21). Sometimes tables were made even stronger by the addition of S-curved braces between the legs and top (cat. 20 and 21).

Song desks, according to paintings such as the *Odes of Bin* (Metropolitan Museum of Art, New York), were often high versions of the Han curved-leg desk. *Composing Poetry on a Spring Outing* (Nelson-Atkins Museum of Art, Kansas City), a painting, attributed to Ma Yuan (active before 1189–after 1225), depicts a large desk with cloud-head feet resting on a continuous-base stretcher. Its design made sitting awkward and is not found in later desks. A standard table, like those in *The Night Revels of Han Xizai,* is the desk for a scribe in Zhang Zeduan's painting, *Spring Festival on the River;* it is the predecessor of the large desk in catalogue number 17. Traditional Chinese desks, or painting tables (*hua'an* or *huazhuo*) as they are called in China, do not have drawers, and writing and painting utensils are stored in separate boxes, cabinets (cat. 26), and the drawers of bookcases (cat. 28). Only in the late Qing (1644–1911), as a result of Western influence, did large desks with many drawers become popular.[11]

Seats

Platforms

In ancient China most people sat and slept on mats, the wealthy and important included, although they also had low platforms on which to sit or recline (fig. 4). A Later Han (25–220 A.D.) pottery tomb relief found near Chengdu, Sichuan, shows respectful, formally dressed students seated in the correct kneeling posture on long rectangular mats and a square single-person mat.[12] The teacher, as befits his status, is elevated on a small, low platform of simple box construction and leans on an armrest In the Han, and throughout Chinese history, seating is arranged according to a complex protocol reflecting social position and having symbolic and sometimes even political implications.

The box-construction form is found as early as the Anyang period of the Shang period on large bronze tables, such as the Duan Fang altar table (Metropolitan Museum of Art, New York). The table has narrow rectangular openings in its sides and is ornamented with alternated dragons in relief. This bronze piece was probably based on a wooden prototype and may have been used to warm sacrificial wine.

Besides boxlike platforms, those supported by legs were also made, and these two types existed together throughout Chinese history. An inscribed stone platform (19 cm high x 87.5 cm wide x 72 cm deep), found in a tomb in Dancheng, Henan, has four recessed legs and spandrels resembling those on the Dangyang sacrificial table (fig. 2).[13] The inscription reads: *Han gu boshi Changshan dazhuan wangjun zuota* (Sitting platform of the deceased Han ruler Erudite Assistant Grand Tutor of Changshan). Thus we know that such platforms were called *ta* and that they were used for sitting. The fact that this *ta* was inscribed with the prince's title and buried in his tomb suggests that *ta* were status symbols used only by high officials.

Square, single-person platforms and long ones for seating several people also existed. The long platforms (*chuang*)[14] were often used with long, curved-leg tables that were placed on the floor in front; they had screens on two sides and sometimes were surmounted by canopies. Any platform of sufficient length could be used as a bed as well as for sitting. In China, beds have always been used as daytime seats and, thus, there is no clear distinction between furniture for sleeping and sitting.

Platforms were frequently equipped with a variety of objects for comfortable daytime living. An Eastern Jin (317–420) pottery tomb model, excavated from tomb number seven at Xiangshan, Nanjing, was found with a pottery armrest, plate, wine cup, ink slab, incense burner, and spittoon.[15] Tang-period paintings from Dunhuang depict large platforms being used as beds or tables or seats for several people. The sides of these platforms have oval openings with cusped or arch-shaped upper edges.

By the tenth century, high wooden platforms like one found in the tomb of Cai Zhuang in Qianjiang, Jiangsu (figs. 6a and 6b), had come into being. In its dimensions, material, and design, this platform resembles furniture used in daily life. However, since it is not strong enough for actual use, it was made expressly for the tomb. It has a gridlike seat on which a mat or thin cushion was placed. The legs, connected by a single side stretcher, have curving profiles ornamented with *ruyi,* auspicious, cloud-head-shaped, wish-fulfilling symbols, which are repeated on the apron. The design imparts a rigidity, flatness, and delicate grace characteristic of the Five Dynasties (907–960) and Song, and distinct from the bold, flowing, three-dimensionality of Ming pieces. In later times, similarly proportioned platforms with four legs continued to be used (cat. 13) as well as very large ones, smaller single-person ones, and box-construction models.

Couch-beds

Ming couch-beds (cat. 14 and 15), which resemble our Western couches but are wider and used for sleeping as well as sitting, evolved from Han-period low platforms with screens on two or three sides. In a stone engraving from a tomb at Anqiu, Shandong, the occupant of the tomb and his wife are each seated on this kind of platform, which has short legs and cusped spandrels (fig. 4). He leans on a curved-leg armrest and holds a large fan. Refreshments are served on low, rectangular tables in front of each platform; wine is ladled from pots elevated on round stands, and acrobats provide entertainment. Four guests are seated on a long platform to one side. Later the platforms acquired high railings on three sides, as may be seen on a painted lacquer screen from the 484 tomb of Sima Jinlong in Datong, Shanxi. Each railing consists of a wooden frame with an inset, cross-hatched panel; the edges of the apron are cut out in wavelike patterns.[16]

When high seats became common the couch assumed new forms. In *The Night Revels of Han Xizai* is seen an unusual U-shaped model, a form that seems to occur only in furniture of this period and one that is derived from the U-shaped pedestals in Buddhist cave temples (fig. 3). The couch, which appears to be lacquered black, has ink paintings inset in the high railings and deep wooden panels on the base. A more open design occurs on a miniature wooden model found at Datong, Shanxi, in the Jin period (1115–1234) tomb of Yan Deyuan, who died in 1190 (fig. 7). The high side and rear railings, originally at the same height with two horizontal bars at the top of each, have open panels with decorative struts. The flat legs are joined by side stretchers and have complex, delicately

Fig. 7. Miniature wooden couch-bed from the Jin period tomb of Yan Deyuan, Datong, Shanxi, 1190. Height 20 cm, width 40.4 cm, depth 25.5 cm.

(Datongshi Bowuguan, "Datong Jindai Yan Deyuan mu fajue jianbao" (Excavation of the Jin Dynasty Tomb of Yan Deyuan at Datong, Shanxi). *Wenwu* 1978.4, p. 5)

Fig. 8. Miniature wooden couch-bed. From the tomb of Zhu Tan, Zhouxian, Ming period, 1389. Shandong Provincial Museum, Jinan.

(J. M. Addis, *Chinese Ceramics from Datable Tombs and Some Other Dated Material: A Handbook.* London and New York: Sotheby Parke Bernet, 1978, p. 65)

Fig. 9. Reproduction of folding bed from tomb no. 2, Baoshan, Jingmen, Hubei. Bed: lacquered wood; railing: bamboo and wood; height 38.4 cm, height of seat 23.6 cm, width 220.8 cm, depth 135.6 cm. Reproduction in Hubei Museum.

(Zhang Yinwu. "A Survey of Chu-Style Furniture." *Journal of the Classical Chinese Furniture Society* 4:3 (Summer 1994), p. 59)

curved edges ending in cloud-head feet. Intrinsically unstable and fragile, cloud-head feet were popular during the Song and Yuan (1279–1368) periods (fig. 6) but do not appear on later hardwood furniture. However, less-pointed variations of the cloud-head foot occur on Qing softwood furniture.[17]

The Jin couch-bed is stiff and somewhat awkward, but by the Ming the design had been perfected and had become a harmonious form. This can be seen as early as 1389 in a wooden model excavated from the tomb of Zhu Tan, the tenth son of the first Ming emperor Taizu (fig. 8). The couch-bed has a low, solid back consisting of three panels, the highest in the center. Each of the slightly lower side railings has one panel. All panels are composed of small, symmetrically arranged, recessed panels that follow the basic structure of the couch-bed. The railings have rounded, butterflied corners that lead the eye down to the smooth outer curves of the cabriole legs. Butterflied corners were used at least as early as the Southern Song (1127–1279), when they appear on the corners of a screen in a fan painting, *A Lady at Her Dressing Table* (Museum of Fine Arts, Boston; fig 12) by Su Hanchen (active c. 1124–63). The base of the couch-bed is waisted and has cabriole legs with interior flanges continuing the line of the curvilinear apron. It is a direct predecessor of the elegantly carved, seventeenth-century version (cat. 15). A low footstool extends the length of the miniature couch-bed and the whole is surrounded by a wooden frame, which undoubtedly supported a curtain that would have been lowered at night for privacy and hooked back during the day when the bed was used for sitting. The frame surrounding the miniature couch-bed is reminiscent of Han-period frames that, on the basis of literary and pictorial evidence, are thought to have been draped with textiles and placed around low platforms.[18]

Canopy beds

Later hardwood canopy beds (cat. 16) evolved from low platforms with lattice railings, examples of which were excavated from fourth century B.C. tombs in the state of Chu. The Chu platforms are sophisticated, beautifully made pieces of furniture. One was found disassembled and neatly stacked against a wall in the 315 B.C. tomb number two at Baoshan, Jingmen, Hubei (fig. 9). This bed consists of two square sections and is hinged so that the fronts and rears fold against the sides. The base is fashioned from wood lacquered black and the railing is constructed of bamboo and wood. Each section of the bed has four legs consisting of spindles fastened to a straight base. The railing has small, rectangular, open panels and is stepped at the openings in the center of each long side. The seat has braces placed along the width and was found spread with a bamboo mat on top of which was a grass mat with a silk-wadded quilt. The linearity of the bed's design is reminiscent of some later hardwood pieces.

Platforms with canopies are shown in Han depictions of ceremonial banquets. However, the first pictorial representation of a canopy bed appears in a stone engraving from a Northern Wei (386–535) tomb. Husband and wife are seated on a bed enclosed by a multipaneled screen with hinged front panels.[19] A similar bedstead can be seen in the painting *The Admonitions of the Instructress to the Court Ladies* (British Museum, London) generally considered to be a close copy of a late-fourth- to early fifth-century composition by Gu Kaizhi. A man is seated on a low, curved-leg bench, like the banquet tables in front of Han ceremonial platforms, looking suggestively at a lady seated within. The bed has a boxlike base with side panels having oval cut-outs with cusped upper edges. The wooden canopy is supported by four corner posts rising from the base and is hung with diaphanous curtains tied up with ribbons. A high, screenlike railing appears to have mat panels on the inside and is hinged so that the bed can be completely enclosed. When the curtains are let down they create a private room within a room. In the Song period the railing became lower and might contain inset ink paintings, as may be seen in the partially visible bedstead at the beginning of *The Night Revels of Han Xizai*. By the Ming, railings with lattice panels were popular (cat. 16, detail).

Stools

Stools comprise a universal and basic type of seat that has been used continuously since ancient times. An early depiction of a high stool, with curved seat and base that widens at the bottom, is found on a fragment of an Eastern Zhou incised-bronze vessel from Liuhe, Jiangsu.[20] Clearly the scene describes a ritual. A man seated on a stool is drinking from a horn-shaped cup. To emphasize the ceremonial nature of the occasion and the man's status and power, the stool is elevated above the usual mat-level height. Folding stools came early to China. On the basis of textual evidence, during the late second century folding stools (*hu chuang*) are thought to have been imported into China via the nomads of the northern border regions. The first pictorial evidence is found on a Buddhist stone stele, whose inscription is dated 543 A.D.[21] Elegant *huanghuali*-wood versions, elevated to chair-level height, are found in the Ming (cat. 2) and the type continues to be used today.

In Buddhist art of the fifth and sixth centuries we find representations of bulbous cane stools, hourglass-shaped stools made from cane or wood, and round

Fig. 10. Detail from a wall painting, Dunhuang cave 285, Western Wei (535–556 A.D.), 538.

(After Tonko Bumbutsu Kenkyu (Dunhuang Research Institute), *Chugoku sekkutsu. Tonko Boko kutsu* (Chinese Cave Temples: The Mogao Caves at Dunhuang). 5 vols. Tokyo: Heibonsha, 1980, vol. 1, plate 146)

wooden stools. Noble ladies of the Tang are frequently portrayed sitting on stools, which were undoubtedly common items of furniture in their homes. The stools are square, round, oval, or hourglass-shaped, and often decorated and used with tasseled cushions. In Song paintings we find the first depictions of round stools that were made from cane bent into circles on the sides. This form influenced the stone and *huanghuali* stools in catalogue numbers 4 and 5.[22]

Chairs

The earliest chairs, like stools, appear in a Buddhist context in China; they were not yet everyday items but honorific seats giving status to important people. A painting in Dunhuang cave 285, dated 538 A.D., shows a meditating monk seated in a kneeling posture on a low armchair with a high back, straight yoke, solid panels beneath the arms, and a woven seat (fig. 10). Such chairs were called "woven seats" (*shengchuang* or *shengzuo*) in sixth-century Buddhist writings. Monks also sat with their legs pendant on high-back chairs without arms, as may be seen in a rubbing from a Buddhist stele, with an inscription dated 566 A.D., in the collection of the late Laurence Sickman. By the Tang period, important officials as well as priests sat on chairs, which the Japanese monk Ennin, in the diary of his travels in China between 838 and 847, refers to by their modern Chinese name *yi*. General Gao Yuangui belonged to an important family and when he died in 756 his high status was indicated by depicting him in a tomb painting seated on a large armchair with protruding crestrail, his feet resting on the floor.[23] An indication of the appearance of an actual Tang chair is provided by a low, wide, Chinese-style armchair in the Shoso-in. Made from zelkova wood, stained red and lacquered, it has square-cut, tapering members, a straight crestrail, a horizontal bar on the back, a low railing around three sides of the seat, and gilded-metal mounts.

Wide armchairs of this type continued to be honorific seats used by Buddhist monks. Examples with curved crestrails made of bamboo or gnarled branches are found in Zhang Shengwen's *Buddhist Images* (National Palace Museum, Taipei), painted between 1173 and 1176. These simple, natural materials create fitting seats for otherworldly monks. An ancient tradition exists in China of imitating the common bamboo in rare and costly materials. An early example is an exquisite censer (Maoling Museum, Xianyang county, Shaanxi) that was excavated from a pit near the tomb of Han Wudi (reigned 140–86 B.C.). It is made of bronze decorated with gold and silver; its long stem was carefully fashioned to resemble a segmented stalk of bamboo.[24] Bamboo, the cheapest and most ordinary of furniture materials, was also sometimes painstakingly imitated in enduring hardwoods (cat. 13). The practice of using another material, be it hardwood or bronze, to imitate bamboo is aesthetically comparable to using naturally crooked wood for furniture. Since at least the sixth century, furniture was made of gnarled wood,[25] and during the Qing period there was a fashion for rootwood furniture (cat. 6).

By the Song period everyone sat on high seats with their legs pendant, and chairs were more widely used and becoming more comfortable and less stiff in appearance. The earliest-known extant Chinese chair was excavated in Julu county, Hebei, from a house that was flooded in 1108.[26] The chair is fashioned from round members; it has splayed legs that are thicker toward the base, a bow-shaped crestrail, and a slight backward arch to the back posts and plain splat. The use of a splat instead of the earlier horizontal rail made the chair more comfortable. Curved spandrels are found beneath the seat; a low stretcher between the front legs probably was originally repeated on the other three sides. Although the workmanship of this chair is apparently a bit rough, the design is a sophisticated forecasting of the so-called "classical" style of Ming-period pieces (cat. 7 and 8). The Hebei chair is similar to the type of sidechair depicted in *The Night Revels of Han Xizai,* which has a curved crestrail with upturned ends over which brocade runners were draped for special occasions (fig. 3).

The armchair with protruding crestrail was the most popular Song chair, but other types were also developed. A back and sometimes horseshoe-shaped arms were added to folding stools to create the folding chair. A folding sidechair and a folding round-back armchair are both depicted in Zhang Zeduan's painting showing daily life in the early twelfth-century capital, *Spring Festival on the River.* By the Ming period, folding armchairs were beautifully decorated (cat. 3) and had become the favored seats for official portraits. The rigid round-back armchair (cat. 11) was also used in Song times and is shown in twelfth-century paintings, such as the handscroll attributed to Fan Long, *The Eighteen Arhats* (Freer Gallery, Washington, D.C.). A miniature pottery armchair of this type was found in the thirteenth-century tomb of Wang Qing in Datong, Shanxi.[27]

Storage Furniture

The earliest storage containers were boxes and chests of various sizes and shapes. It was only with the adoption of the chair-level mode of living that cabinets developed. Boxes, however, never lost their appeal and continued to be used in the study, on picnics, in the sedan chair, and stacked in the bedroom. Storage furniture was always provided with locks, at least since the Tang period, when beautifully crafted examples were made.

An early depiction of a cabinet is found at the end of a Southern Song handscroll that shows the processes involved in sericulture[28] (fig. 11). The cabinet stands on a table and has a truncated, pyramid-shaped top identical to lids found on boxes since the first century A.D.[29] The upper parts of the wood-hinged doors have lattice panels, one of which has been left open to reveal a central shelf. The cabinet, with its short feet and standard apron, is a predecessor of the higher, tapered cabinets of the Ming (cat. 26 and 27). Although there are no extant pre-Ming Chinese cabinets,[30] the pivoted-door construction has been used since at least the Western Zhou period (eleventh century–771 B.C.), which is attested to by a bronze *fangli,* a combination stove and cooking vessel.[31] One door of the bronze vessel has a small, naked, crouching man holding a bar that fits

Fig. 11. Anonymous. Detail of *Sericulture,* Southern Song.
Handscroll, ink and color on silk; height 27.5 cm × width
513 cm. Heilongjiang Provincial Museum.

(After *Zhongguo meishu quanji: huihua bian 4: Liang Song
huihua* (The Great Treasury of Chinese Fine Arts.
Painting Section, vol. 4: Painting of the Two Song
Dynasties), plate 21)

into a *taotie*-ornamented ring on the other door. This method of closing the
doors is a precursor of that found on Ming cabinets, where the barlike lock
passes through rings on the doors and stile.

In his poem, "On a Box Containing His Own Works," the Tang poet Bo Juyi
(772–846) writes about a cypress-wood book-box that he made for his collected
works. He also describes a monumental octagonal, revolving bookcase for storing
the *Tripitaka* at the Nan Chan Temple in Suzhou, in which the scriptures were
kept behind closed doors. Only in the Northern Song (960–1126) do we begin
to find high, open-shelved bookcases, such as a rustic model shown in a wall
painting in Kaihua Temple, Gaoping County, Shaanxi.[32] Later hardwood bookcases
were often elegant pieces of furniture with drawers beneath the middle shelf and
low railings on three sides (cat. 28).

Screens, Stands, and Racks

Screens are important pieces of furniture used for protection against drafts, for
room-dividing privacy, to shield women from the gaze of men, and to honor
those seated in front of them. Since they are often very decorative and display
calligraphy, poetry, and painting—the highest art forms in China—they have a
uniquely elevated position in the realm of furniture.

A number of miniature painted-lacquer screens unearthed from Chu tombs in
modern Jiangling, Hubei, show that screens were profusely ornamented as early as
the Warring States period. One of these is a long, low model with a complex
openwork design of fifty-five intertwining snakes, frogs, deer, and birds. During the
Han period screens became higher and narrower, with solid panels decorated
with dragons, scrolls, or geometric patterns. Elaborately carved, gilt-bronze mounts
and supports, which once embellished a large three-panel screen, were found in
the tomb of the king of Nanyue in Xianggang, Guangzhou, Guangdong. Screens
consisting of a long back panel and one short side panel are frequently shown

around platforms (fig. 4). Besides protecting and concealing, screens performed an honorific function by isolating and enhancing the person to whom homage was being paid. In the Han imperial palace the screens sometimes were painted with historical scenes intended as models of good conduct and warnings to the emperor and his ladies against improper behavior.

The earliest extant remains of a complete paneled screen were excavated at Datong, Shanxi, from the 484 A.D. tomb of Sima Jinlong. Five wooden panels decorated with lacquer paintings illustrating stories of virtuous women were found together with four stone bases, suggesting that the screen had been stationary. Perhaps it had two side wings. By the fourth century A.D., paneled screens with hinged front panels were used on canopy beds, and screens were decorated with paintings by Gu Kaizhi and other famous artists. At first, artists painted directly on the wooden panels, but during the Tang it became common for the paintings to be done on silk or paper and then mounted on the screen. Favorite poems were written on screens, or their paintings might illustrate lines of poetry. Each panel of a famous six-panel screen from the Shoso-in has a sketch of a beautiful Tang lady beneath a tree, done in ink and light colors and originally embellished with pheasant feathers. The paintings are done on paper, which was mounted on ramie cloth and attached to wooden frames joined together by cords.

With the advent of the chair-level mode of living in the Northern Song, screens became much larger and framed panels fitted into slots in massive feet, just as in extant Ming and Qing hardwood screens (fig. 3 and cat. 1). Single-panel and folding screens were decorated with works by the greatest landscape and bird-and-flower painters of the time. The Song witnessed a fashion for large wave paintings mounted on single-panel screens, as may be seen in Su Hanchen's fan painting, *A Lady at Her Dressing Table*. Sometimes a number of small paintings were mounted together on a screen.

Small, single-panel screens, called "pillow screens" (*zhenping*), were used to shelter a sleeper from drafts, just as in the Han period, but in the Song the bed was a raised platform rather than a mat on the floor. When placed on the desk, small screens were called "inkstone screens" (*yanping*). According to the thirteenth-century connoisseur Zhao Xigu, they were invented by Su Shi (1037–1101) and Huang Tingjian (1042–1105) to display inkstone inscriptions. Also set into screens were wonderfully figured marble panels, which often evoked a landscape painting.[33]

Screenlike forms also support mirrors. The top of some mirror stands are reminiscent of the elaborate five-panel, stationary screens that were placed behind thrones. Chinese mirrors are round and made of bronze; one side is polished while the other is decorated and has a raised knob in the center through which a cord is threaded for hanging. When people sat on mats, mirrors were set on the top of polelike stands. An early depiction, on a lacquer dish from a tomb datable to 249 A.D., shows that the stand has a shelf in the middle of the pole and

Fig. 12. Su Hanchen (twelfth century), *A Lady at Her Dressing Table*. Fan painting, ink and colors on silk; height 25.2 cm x width 26.7 cm. Ross Collection, Museum of Fine Arts, Boston (29.960).

Fig. 13. Detail of a wall painting from a tomb in Baisha, Henan, 1099.

(After Su Bai, *Baisha Song mu* (Song Tombs at Baisha). Beijing: Wenwu Press, 1957, plate 27)

a large base for stability.[34] During the Song, mirror stands were elevated on high tables and assumed new forms. In a boudoir scene from a wall painting in a 1099 tomb in Baisha, Henan, a mirror is suspended by its cord from a finial at the top of a rectangular stand with *ruyi* ornamenting the upturned ends of its curved crestrail and low cloud-head feet (fig. 13). Here the mirror hangs perpendicular, but on most stands it is supported at an angle. A lacquer folding stand of this type was excavated near Fuzhou in Fujian province from the mid-thirteenth-century tomb of the seventeen-year-old wife of the county magistrate.[35] How the young lady might have used it can be seen in Su Hanchen's *A Lady at Her Dressing Table*. A fanciful variation of the folding stand is an exquisitely fashioned silver one in the shape of a folding chair, which was buried in 1365 in the tomb of Cao Si, Zhang Shicheng's mother.[36] Another mirror stand shaped like a protruding-crestrail armchair, and thus not folding, is depicted in a fan painting, *Morning Toilette in the Women's Quarters*, (National Palace Museum, Taipei), attributed to Wang Shen (b. 1036).

Mirror stands were often placed on top of small chests with drawers. An early wooden example of this type was found in a Southern Song tomb in Cunqian, Wujin, Jiangsu.[37] It consists of two drawers beneath a tray with a removable lid. Inside the tray is a collapsible stand that would have supported the mirror.

In addition to mirror stands, the bedroom was furnished with a garment rack and a washbasin stand. Garment racks were the equivalent of modern-day clothes closets, except that instead of concealing the garments behind a door, the Chinese built attractive racks that display them. Garment racks were placed beside the bed, as can be seen at the beginning of *The Night Revels of Han Xizai*, where the upturned ends of a rack draped with a red garment are visible beyond the bed curtain (fig. 3). A garment rack of essentially the same form as Ming examples is depicted in a second-century A.D. stone engraving in a tomb in Yi'nan, Shandong.[38] It is a simple post-and-rail form, decorated with geometric patterns. In the Song wall paintings at Baisha, larger garment racks are depicted with upturned *ruyi*-shaped crestrails and *ruyi*-ornamented spandrels.[39] Later hardwood garment racks are often more elaborately ornamented with complex openwork carvings (cat. 29).

Narrow variations of the garment rack were used for towels in the washing area. A Baisha painting shows such a rack with a fringed towel hanging over its crestrail (fig. 13). In front of the towel rack a blue washbasin rests on a stand with cabriole legs. Previously, washbasins were placed on the floor or slightly elevated on low legs, like the one carried by a painted terra-cotta figurine of a female attendant found in the tomb of Zhang Sheng, who was buried in 595 in modern Anyang, Henan.[40] By the Ming period the towel rack and washbasin stand were combined into elegant, sophisticated pieces of furniture.

The history of China's furniture, like its architecture, is the history of beauty merged with function. The Chinese developed every basic furniture type: for sleeping, storing, sitting, eating, and working. They also made other practical household pieces: screens, mirror stands, garment racks, and washbasin stands. The Chinese cabinetmaker created these objects with lines, proportions, and decorations that often transformed them into beautiful art objects permitting graceful living. More than paintings, rugs, and tableware, which are displayed and removed according to occasion and season, these furniture pieces give a fixed structure of beauty to a Chinese room. The functional heart of beauty in a Chinese house is wood shaped and standing through the winds of time.

Notes

1. Jessica Rawson, *Western Zhou Ritual Bronzes from the Arthur M. Sackler Collections*. Washington, D.C.: Arthur M. Sackler Foundation, 1992, p. 370, plate 40.2.

2. Lin Shouqin. *Zhanguo ximugong sunjie he gongyi yabjiu* (The Craft of Tenon Making in Fine Woodwork during the Warring States Period). Hong Kong: Chinese University Press, 1981.

3. Wang Shixiang, *Classic Chinese Furniture: Ming and Early Qing Dynasties*. Trans. by Sarah Handler and the author. San Francisco: China Books & Periodicals, 1986, p. 36.

4. Mary Fong, "The Origin of Chinese Pictorial Representation of the Human Figure." *Artibus Asiae* XLIX, 1/2 (1988), figs. 2 and 4.

5. Henansheng Wenwu Yanjiusuo (Cultural Relics Institute of Henan Province). *Xinyang chumu* (The Chu Tombs at Xinyang). Beijing: Wenwu Press, 1986, plate XXVII.1.

6. Ibid., plate XXVII.4.

7. Anhuisheng Wenwu Kaogu Yanjiuso and Tianchang Xian Wenwu Guanliso (Institute of Cultural Relics of Anhui Province and CPAM, Tianchang County), "Anhui Tianchang xian Sanjiaowei Zhanguo Xi Han mu chutu" (The Cultural Relics Unearthed from Tombs of the Warring States Period to the Western Han Dynasty at Sanjiaowei in Tianchang County, Anhui). *Wenwu* 1993.9, p. 24.

8. Tonko Bumbutsu Kenkyu (Dunhuang Research Institute), *Chugoku sekkutsu. Tonko Boko kutsu* (Chinese Cave Temples: The Mogao Caves at Dunhuang). 5 vols. Tokyo: Heibonsha, 1980, vol. 4, p. 157.

9. Wang Renbo, ed. *Sui Tang Wenhua* (Culture of the Sui and Tang Dynasties). Hong Kong: China Books, 1990, pp. 200–201.

10. Reproduced on cover of *Wenwu* 1962.10.

11. Small tables with drawers were also sometimes used as desks. In an illustration of a silk shop in the Chongzhen (1628–44) edition of the novel *Jin Ping Mei* (The Plum in the Golden Vase), we see the back of what, because of its construction, must be a small table with drawers used as a desk by the shopkeeper (André Lévy, trans. *Fleur en Fiole d'Or* (*Jin Ping Mei cihua*). 15 vols. Paris: Gallimard, 1983, vol. 2, chpt. 60, p. 242). Li Yu (1610/11–80) was obsessed with the usefulness of drawers and advocated having them in writing tables (Li Yu. *Yijiayen zhong zhi juchi qiwan* (Independent Words: The Section on Useful and Decorative Objects in the Dwelling). Beijing: Zhongguo Yingzuo Xueshe, 1931, p. 25b). A clear reference to a small table with drawers, which was used as a desk, is found in chapter eighty-one of the mid-eighteenth-century novel *The Story of the Stone* (David Hawkes and John Minford, trans. *The Story of the Stone*. 5 vols. Harmondsworth, Eng.: Penguin, 1976–86, vol. 4, p. 49).

12. Lucy Lim, ed., *Stories from China's Past: Han Dynasty Pictorial Tomb Reliefs and Archaeological Objects from Sichuan Province, People's Republic of China*. San Francisco: Chinese Cultural Center, 1987, p. 122.

13. Cao Guicen. "Henan Dancheng Han shi ta" (A Han Stone Platform from Dancheng, Henan). *Kaogu* 1965.5, p. 258.

14. In *Tongsu wen* (Popular Literature), the Later Han writer Fu Qian distinguishes between *ta*, which are 84 cm (3 feet, 5 inches) long; *ping*, or boards on which one person could sit; and *chuang*, which are 192 cm (8 feet) long. (Chen Menglei, ed., *Gujin tushu jicheng* (Imperially Commissioned Compendium of Literature and Illustrations, Ancient and Modern). 1726. Reprint edition: Shanghai: Zhongguo Shuju, 1934, vol. 797, *juan* 215, p. 49a.)

15. Chen Zengbi. "Qian nian gu ta" (A Thousand-Year-Old *Ta*). *Wenwu* 1984.6, p. 67.

16. *Wenhua dageming qijian chudu wenwu* (Cultural Relics Unearthed During the Period of the Great Cultural Revolution). Beijing: Wenwu Press, 1972, p. 144.

17. See Nancy Berliner and Sarah Handler, *Friends of the House: Furniture from China's Towns and Villages*. Salem, Mass.: Peabody Essex Museum, 1996.

18. Sarah Handler, "A Little World Made Cunningly: The Chinese Canopy Bed." *Journal of the Classical Chinese Furniture Society* 2:2 (Spring 1992), pp. 6–7.

19. Toshio Nagahiro, *Representational Art of the Six Dynasties Period*. Tokyo: Bijutsu Shuppan-sha, 1969, p. 73.

20. Charles D. Weber, *Chinese Pictorial Bronze Vessels of the Late Chou Period*. Ascona, Switzerland: Artibus Asiae, 1968, p. 45.

21. Wu Tung, "From Imported 'Nomadic Seat' to Chinese Folding Armchair." *Boston Museum of Fine Arts Bulletin* LXXI (1973).363, pp. 39, 46, fig. 11.

22. Sarah Handler, "The Ubiquitous Stool." *Journal of the Classical Chinese Furniture Society* 4:3 (Summer 1994), pp. 6–11.

23. Ho Zicheng, "Tang mu bihua" (Tang Tomb Paintings). *Wenwu* 1959.8, p. 33.

24. *Jinguo chutu wenwu zhenpin xuan* (A Selection of the Treasures of Archaeological Finds of the People's Republic of China, 1976–1984). Beijing: Wenwu Press, 1987, plates 225–27.

25. Mette Siggstedt, "Chinese Root Furniture." *Bulletin of the Museum of Far Eastern Antiquities* 63 (1991), p. 146.

26. Louise Hawley Stone, *The Chair in China*. Toronto: Royal Ontario Museum of Archaeology, 1952, p. 19.

27. "Shanxi sheng Datong shi Yuandai Feng Daozhen, Wang Qing mu qingli jianbao" (Report on the Yuan Dynasty Tombs of Feng Daozhen and Wang Qing at Datong City, Shanxi Province). *Wenwu Cankao Ziliao* 1962.10, p. 44.

28. *Zhongguo meishu quanji huihua bian 4: Liang Song hui-hua* (The Great Treasury of Chinese Fine Arts. Painting Section, vol. 4: Painting of the Two Song Dynasties). Beijing: Xinhua Shudian, 1988, p. 21.

29. Zeng Zhaoyu, et al. *Yinan gu huaxiangshi mu fajue baogao* (A Report on the Excavation of the Decorated Tomb at Yinan). Shanghai: Cultural Administrative Bureau, 1956, plate 51.

30. A red-lacquered zelkova-wood cabinet, which was made before 687, is in the Shoso-in. It is, however, very different in material, construction, and design from any known Chinese cabinets. (Shosoin Office, ed. *Treasures of the Shosoin*. Tokyo: Asahi Shimbun, 1965, plate 72.)

31. Danielie and Vadime Elisseff, *New Discoveries in China: Encountering History Through Archeology*. New York: Chartwell, 1983, p. 58.

32. Sarah Handler, "Cabinets and Shelves Containing All Things in China." *Journal of the Classical Chinese Furniture Society* 4:1 (Winter 1993), pp. 9–11.

33. Sarah Handler, "The Chinese Screen: Movable Walls to Divide, Enhance, and Beautify." *Journal of the Classical Chinese Furniture Society* 3:3 (Summer 1993), pp. 4–18.

34. Yang Hong, "Sanguo kaogu de xin faxian" (New Archaeological Finds from the Three Kingdoms). *Wenwu* 1986.3, color plate 1.

35. Fuzhousheng Bowuguan. *Fuzhou Nan Song Huang Pu Mu* (The Southern Song Tomb of Huang Pu in Fuzhou). Beijing: Wenwu Press, 1982, plate 73.

36. *Gems of China's Cultural Relics 1992*. Beijing: Wenwu Press, 1992, plate 138.

37. Wang Shixiang, *Connoisseurship of Chinese Furniture: Ming and Early Qing Dynasties*. 2 vols. Trans. by Wang Shixiang, Lark E. Mason, Jr., et al. Hong Kong: Joint Publishing, 1990, vol. 1, p. 98.

38. Zeng Zhaoyu, et al., p. 79.

39. Su Bai, *Baisha Song mu* (Song Tombs at Baisha). Beijing: Wenwu Press, 1957, plates 25 and 37.

40. Elisseff, p. 167.

Fig. 8. Inkline.

The Furniture Maker and the Woodworking Traditions of China

Curtis Evarts

Little has been recorded about the production of furniture during the late Ming and early Qing periods, or about the craftsmen who fashioned it. In the West, where the individual and his talents are celebrated, the makers of fine furniture and other decorative works of art are frequently identifiable, but the lives and practices of Chinese artisans were rarely documented. Although the literati signed their paintings and poems, the members of the artisan class generally remained anonymous outside of their immediate circles. In this essay, I hope to shed some light on furniture making in China—who made it and how they made it—by exploring its specific traditions within the broader context of woodworking.

Historical Perspective

The earliest literary sources indicate that carpenters were highly respected members of the general artisan class. The ability to realize artistic creation through meditative states is venerated by Zhuangzi, who records the tale of the master bell-frame maker who fasted for weeks, not daring to waste his *qi,* until at last he envisioned the completed work while gazing at the bough of a tree.[1] In Chinese classical literature, carpentry tools—with their functions of guiding and measuring—served as metaphors for virtuous and moral lives,[2] and during the Warring States period (475–221), these emblems of integrity and uprightness were part of the grave furnishings of the nobility.[3] Finally, Liu Sheng's second-century B.C. "Ode to Fine-Grained Wood" demonstrates the Chinese love for utilitarian objects crafted of beautifully figured woods.

> Whether made into a wooden pillow or table,
> wood with excellent fine grain is a guarantee of splendid poems,
> and the composition of perfect documents.[4]

By the Song period (960–1279), architectural styles that were to last through the Ming (1368–1644) and Qing (1644–1911) periods were already well established. Detailed drawings of timber-frame joinery illustrated in the *Yingzao fashi* (Treatise on Architectural Methods), compiled in 1097, clearly document the sophistication that woodworking had achieved at that period. Here the basic division between rough carpentry, or literally, "large carpentry" (*da muzuo*), and that of more refined woodworking, or "small carpentry," is also first recorded. In architectural terms, rough carpentry included the shaping and assembly of beams, columns, and roof-frame members into building structures. The more refined process of woodworking was associated with the fabrication of the lattice panels, windows, doors, interior partitions, carved decorations, and balustrades that were fitted into the modular timber-frame structures, as well as of the furniture that was arranged within.

Two major divisions of furniture construction—recessed-leg and corner-leg—were well established by the Song period. The recessed-leg style appears to have been derived from post-and-beam architecture. Reduced to a smaller scale in furniture making, the basic technique revolves around a horizontal mitered frame (be it for a seat, tabletop, or cabinet top) and four legs, which were joined at points inset—or "recessed"—from the corners of the top frame. The legs splay outward toward the base, and are connected by various configurations of stretchers and/or aprons. Scenes of wine shops and restaurants from the Song painting *Qingming shanghetu* (Spring Festival on the River), as well as archaeological finds of contemporary furniture, suggest that recessed-leg tables, chairs, and stools were widely used during the Song period (cf. cat. 17 and 18).

The waisted form of furniture retains characteristics of the classical Greek pedestal that migrated eastward to Gandhara where, as a dignified support, it became associated with the seat of Buddha (*xumizuo*). As Buddhism spread into China, so did the classical pedestal form.[5] Generally speaking, throughout the Song period waisted tables were used for religious or ceremonial purposes, and waisted platforms were reserved for priests and those of high status. During the Ming period, waisted furniture shed its base stretchers and developed into an elegant, open form that eventually lost its religious and ceremonial significance and was assimilated into the basic repertoire of furniture types (cf. cat. 9 and 20).

In 1567 a ban on imports was lifted, thus stimulating trade along the coastal regions. The fashionableness of furniture made from imported tropical hardwoods was noted by Fan Lian in 1593:

> When I was young I never saw a single piece of hardwood furniture, such as a writing table or meditation chair. The common people only used brown-lacquered square tables made from ginkgo wood....During the Longqing [1567–72] and Wanli [1573–1620] periods, even the lower *yamen* servants began to use fine wooden furniture.[6]

During the prosperous early to middle Qing period, the Yongzheng (1723–35) and Qianlong (1736–96) emperors, who had a strong interest in the wide range of artisan crafts, also encouraged the development of new furniture designs in the imperial workshops. The end of the Yongzheng reign period, however, is generally used to mark the close of the end of the golden age of Chinese furniture making. Under the powerful influence of Qianlong, the refined classical patterns that had evolved from the Song period degenerated into elaborate, fanciful forms that were in accordance with his stylistic preference for the archaic design. Thus, the golden age of furniture making is considered to be the late Ming and early Qing periods, during which unprecedented heights were achieved, and beautiful materials were combined with integrated structure and balanced design. Today it is recognized as one of the world's greatest traditions in the decorative arts.

Organization of Labor

Although little is recorded about individual craftsmen, it is known that artisans were organized into guilds as early as the Song period.[7] Karl Marx compared the formation of guilds to an evolutionary process in nature that "regulates the differentiation of plants and animals into species and varieties."[8] Highly protective of their specialized skills, the familylike guilds in China were able to control competition, ensure some semblance of welfare for their members, and set up their own process of "natural selection" by instituting rigorous controls for training through the system of apprenticeships to master craftsmen. A son may have learned directly from his father, or have been apprenticed to relatives, associates, or friends in nearby villages. The apprenticeship usually entailed surviving a lengthy, demeaning, and slaverylike novitiate, after which basic skills were gradually transmitted to the apprentice, who may have augmented his meager education by furtively observing a superior journeyman at work. A 1948 study of apprenticeships in Chengdu noted:

> He does things from his own observation exactly as done by his *shifu* (master). Even the details must be followed to the letter. In most cases even the asking of a question is not allowed...even verbal transmissions are sometimes not present.[9]

Guilds collected taxes from members for payment to the imperial treasuries, and organized the yearly imposed-labor service. They also sponsored annual celebrations in honor of their guardian deities; for woodworkers, this was the immortalized Lu Ban.

The first written documentation of furniture making traditions appears during the Ming period, in the carpenter's manual *Lu Ban Jing* (The Classic of Lu Ban). The text of the *Lu Ban Jing* is generally thought to be a work of the fifteenth century, with sections copied from earlier Yuan (1279–1368) sources.[10] A reference in the introduction suggests that it may have been a by-product of the Yongle reign period (1403-24), during which an imperial palace was established at the new northern capital of Beijing, requiring large-scale organization and mobilization of craftsmen and workshops.

> When in the Yongle period of our Ming dynasty the imperial palace was erected in Peking, the ten thousand corvee workers relied without exception, full of awe, on the divine guidance of the master, and only then did they succeed in completing the work.[11]

The omission from the text of mention of the popular tropical hardwoods that had become so popular in the late sixteenth century, while other indigenous materials such as camphor, *nanmu,* and fir are mentioned, thus likely places the *Lu Ban Jing* as a mid-Ming publication.

At that time, artisans throughout the country were required to register and then to work at the new capital either as resident artisans (*zhuzuo gongjiang*) or as shift artisans (*lunban gongjiang*). Resident artisans, as the name implies, resided in the capital and contributed their talents for ten days each month. Shift artisans traveled from all over the country to report for three months of corvee duty each three years. These journeys to the distant capital and the resultant loss of earning power imposed great hardships on the artisans and their families. Nevertheless, the enforced corvee duty had the macrodynamic effect of disseminating broadly the specialized knowledge that was concentrated at the capital, and was likely responsible for unifying woodworking styles and techniques throughout China. The hardships suffered and the intolerable working conditions, however, eventually incited so much protest within the ranks of labor that, after 1562, reporting in person for corvee service was abolished in lieu of paying a tax in silver. After the fall of the Ming period, the registration of craftsmen was abolished.[12] The new freedom of craftsmen to set up their own commercial shops, coupled with the opening of China to foreign trade in 1567, proved to foster a climate in which the craft industries, including that of furniture making, flourished.

With the prosperity of the early Qing period came the revitalization of the imperial workshops. The most talented craftsmen were sought throughout the country to produce jades, porcelains, lacquer wares, cloisonnés, bronzes, and other objects. The production of the imperial woodworking shops, following the tradition of *xiao muzuo* (small woodworking), included partitions, mosquito tents, screens, decorated coverings, and windows, as well as a wide variety of lacquered and hardwood furniture. Records from the Yongzheng imperial workshops indicate that the best furniture craftsmen were recruited from Guangzhou and Suzhou[13] and were generally supervised by talented eunuchs or officials who were in direct contact with the emperor.

Division of Labor

In woodworking, as well as many other craft industries in China, division of labor has been a longstanding practice. A single finished piece of porcelain may have passed through as many as seventy different hands.[14] An acquaintance of the author, who traveled by foot through remote areas in central China during the 1930s, recently recalled his wonder at coming across a group of cartwrights working with simple handtools in an assembly line process. Several workers were relegated to spoke production, more highly skilled joiners fit together the curved segments of the wheel and fashioned the hub, while wheel assemblers completed the process at the end.[15] Plank sawyers, working twelve hours a day on a diet of rice three times a day, have also remained a breed of their own, even into the twentieth century,[16] and continue to follow traditions established nearly one thousand years ago. The chapter entitled "Saw Works: Merit for Cutting," in the *Yingzao fashi,* sets forth the sawyer's rates, based on linear footage of board production relative to the species of wood being cut. The softer the wood, the more footage required for equivalent *gong* (merit) or payment:

(1) oak (*zhou*), or sandalwood (*tan*), *li* [17] fifty feet (*chi*)

(2) miscellaneous hardwoods like elm (*yu*) or locust (*huai*), fifty-five feet

(3) white pine (*baisong mu*), seventy feet

(4) softwoods like *nan* and cypress (*bo*) seventy-five feet

(5) elm (*yu*),[18] yellow pine (*huangsong*), water pine (*shuisong*), and yellow-heart wood(*huangxin*), eighty feet

(6) fir (*shan*) or [*wu*]*tong*, one hundred feet.

(7) A 10 percent adjustment is made for sawing single lengths over twenty feet (2 *zhang*), or for sawing old inferior [reused] material full of nails.[19]

It is interesting to note here the clear reference to the reuse of old materials, indicating that this was a common practice by the Song period. This passage and others illustrate the level of specialization and division of labor in the building trades that was already well established by the tenth century.

By the late seventeenth century, the woodworking trade was highly specialized. "[M]ast, oar, and table [makers] all have their experts," wrote Pu Songling (1640–1715) in his collagelike poem on carpentry. His stanzas go on to describe the vocations of timber carpenters and skilled joiners, who crafted a range of traditional woodworkers' products, including irrigation and waterworks equipment ("flood gates, which must be as well crafted as dowry furniture"). Carvers specialized in signs and tablets, architectural elements, and devotional figures.[20]

Modern studies have shown that divisions were also found among woodcarvers, who specialized in three-dimensional carving, high-relief carving, low-relief carving, or open carving. Moreover, production carving was divided between rough carvers and finish carvers, who usually worked together one-on-one, as a team. The rough carver, who was generally the elder and possessed a comprehensive knowledge of traditional designs, was responsible for conceptualizing and roughing out the general designs. Finish carvers refined and smoothed the surfaces and added the fine detailing.[21] A modern study of the art-carved furniture industry in Hong Kong has established a ratio of four rough carvers : four finish carvers : three joiners : one finisher among woodworkers still using handtools.[22] Of course, both Cantonese-style furniture and Shanghai-style furniture are generally more heavily carved than "classical," late-Ming-style furniture. Nevertheless, this ratio would be likely to apply to finely carved pieces like the *chuang* and canopy bed (cat. 15 and 16) in this exhibition, and regardless of today's aesthetic preference, the additional labor required would justify a considerably higher value placed upon such pieces.

Pu Songling lists other specialists in furniture production. Seat weavers were required, for "chairs, *chuang*s, platforms (*ta*), and stools," as were finishers who used "wood files and sharkskin [to prepare surfaces for] repeated coats of oil and lacquer mixed with ashes." Itinerant woodworkers repaired old furniture, and "when joints became loose or broken, they were re-wedged to make them strong and firm....And there is also [the realm of] bamboo craftsmen; [whether it be for] bridges or *chuang*s, all use bamboo wrapped with split cane."[23]

Another fascinating offshoot of furniture making was centered in the Tiantai Mountains of Zhejiang province, a region well known for its Buddhist/Daoist-inspired root furniture made of gnarled and twisted rattan (see cat. 6).[24] Perhaps completely outside of Lu Ban's domain was the production of garden furniture made of stone (see cat. 4) and porcelain.

The fashioning and mounting of metal hardware appears to have been another specialized division of labor distinct from the woodworking tradition. There are no references to metal mounts (excluding nails) in the *Lu Ban Jing*, which nevertheless is rich in references to specific wooden parts. Moreover, the fact that surface-mounted hardware is often rather crudely fastened suggests that fittings were installed by someone other than a woodworker who specialized in producing carefully fitted joints and smooth surfaces. In addition, the placement of the hardware on many lacquered cabinets shows little regard for the inlaid designs,[25] suggesting an assembly line process that, in its final stages, passed the otherwise completed pieces of furniture to a metalsmith.

Workshop Specialization

A systematic overview of the surviving pieces of late-Ming and early Qing hardwood furniture has confirmed the existence of several specialized workshops in which basic furniture models were individualized with decorative variations. Thus the workshop origins of several groups of chairs have been identified, based upon underlying construction patterns and molded profiles.[26] In addition to these published groups, another group including several *huanghuali,* low-back, southern official's armchairs (a pair published by Wang,[27] one in the collection of the Central Academy of Arts, Beijing,[28] and one in a private collection in Honolulu) and two pairs of *huanghuali* round-back armchairs[29] (private collection, Hong Kong) also appear to have been patterned upon a single prototype.

Canopy beds, considered part of the standard dowry furniture, also appear to have been produced by specialty workshops. Based on a number of extant beds following prototype designs, two such workshops have now been identified. For example, a bed in the Museum of Classical Chinese Furniture, made of *huanghuali* and elegantly refined in the Suzhou-style tradition,[30] is of nearly identical design and construction to two beds—one in red lacquer and one in *jumu*—known to have come from the Suzhou area. Although the materials and finishes differ, their distinctive decorative motifs and construction techniques signify the work of a single workshop.

The bed illustrated in figure 1 is one of a larger group of *huanghuali* beds that appear to have been produced by a specialized workshop in northern China. Similar examples include those in the Great Mosque in Xian, the Palace Museum in Beijing,[31] the San Antonio Museum of Art (fig. 2), and one known to be in a private collection in Beijing.[32] If the beds of this group were to be stripped of their secondary decorative elements, nearly identical superstructures would reveal the following characteristics: (1) the posts are typically square in section, with rounded or indented corners; (2) the short sides of the surrounding upper-panel frameworks typically drop below the long rectangular frame and are shaped with an ogival profile (figs. 3a and 3b); (3) these upper panels are visually supported by open-carved spandrels of immature dragons, with longer spandrels at the front that extend through grooves in the entry posts; (4) also typical of this group are high-waisted platforms fit with bamboo struts and decorative *taohuan* panels; and (5) cabriole legs, some of which are additionally carved with animal masks and claw feet.

Moreover, now that construction techniques particular to the superstructure

Fig. 1. Canopy bed, seventeenth century. *Huanghuali,* height 225.1 cm, length 226.1 cm, width 156.4 cm. Museum of Classical Chinese Furniture, Renaissance, Cailifornia.

Figs. 3a, b. Detail of spandrels: (a) after Fig. 1; (b) similar detail from cat. 16.

Fig. 2. A Chinese Ming-period, six-post canopy bed, early seventeenth century. *Huanghuali,* height 236.2 cm, length 201.9 cm, width 152.4 cm. Collection of the San Antonio Museum of Art, Gift of Bessie Timon (65.111.34/444).

have been identified, two additional beds with variously styled platforms can now be considered as part of this group. The bed in this exhibition (cat. 16), as well as another in a private Hong Kong collection, have identical primary upper structures, which fall into the basic family described above. Based on their decorative style and the generous use of materials, three of the eight beds in this group (Table A)—those in Xian, in the Palace Museum, and in Hong Kong—appear to be a generation or more earlier than the two beds illustrated in figures 1 and 2. We might thus hypothesize that a single workshop produced prototype beds over several generations.

Table A

	Location	Dating	Platform	Secondary Decoration
1	Palace Museum, Beijing	sixteenth/ seventeenth centuries	cabriole leg	dense pattern of lattice-work panels with a texture resembling brocade
2	Great Mosque, Xian	sixteenth/ seventeenth centuries	cabriole leg	dense lattice-work panels; texture resembling brocade, perhaps with some Islamic influence
3	Private collection, Hong Kong	sixteenth/ seventeenth centuries	C-curved leg	dense lattice-work panels; texture resembling brocade, perhaps with some Islamic influence
4	Museum of Fine Arts, Boston, exhibition	seventeenth century	cabriole leg	richly textured patterns of round longevity characters (*yuanshou*) and single-leg dragons (*kuilong*), with frontal panels carved with *qilins*
5	Private collection, Taiwan	seventeenth/ eighteenth centuries	cabriole leg with *sichi tuntou*	richly textured patterns of round longevity characters and single-leg dragons, with frontal panels carved with *shou* and *fu* characters
6	Museum of Classical Chinese Furniture	seventeenth/ eighteenth centuries	cabriole leg with *sichi tuntou*	richly textured patterns of round longevity characters and single-leg dragons, with frontal panels carved with *qilins*
7	San Antonio Museum of Art	seventeenth/ eighteenth centuries	cabriole leg with *sichi tuntou*	richly textured patterns of round longevity characters and single-leg dragons
8	Private collection, Beijing	seventeenth/ eighteenth centuries	cabriole leg	lattice railings with cloud-shaped *ruyi* medallions interspersed with birds and floral motifs, imparting an overall feeling of femininity

Individuality is achieved in this group of canopy beds through variety in the open-carved panels and lattice designs. The bed in figure 1 features richly textured patterns of round longevity characters (*yuanshou*) and single-leg dragons (*kuilong*), with frontal panels carved with *qilins*. The panels of the privately owned Beijing bed are more delicately carved with birds, flowers, and phoenixes. The dense latticework panels of the beds in Hong Kong and at the Great Mosque of Xian have a texture resembling brocade perhaps with some Islamic influence. In the last three years, this author has also noted four *huanghuali* twelve-panel screens with variously decorated, open-carved panels contained within prototype frameworks. In all these examples, the woodworking joiner was bound to the reproduction of model forms, while the lattice specialist and carver demonstrated their artistic license through infinite variations upon recurring themes.

An efficient system of distribution and merchandising supported a high level of workshop specialization. A depiction of a furniture shop filled with high-quality household furnishings, in a documentary painting (d. 1770) of Qianlong's southern tour (fig. 4), may serve to illustrate this point. Established along a major canal route in a thriving city, this shop appears to function as an outlet for canopy beds, cabinets and wardrobes, sets of chairs and stools, benches, garment racks, altar tables, and square tables.[33] The system of canals in China has provided an extensive network for the distribution of goods for centuries. Today one can still witness the steady stream of barges, now powered with diesel engines, puttering up and down the Grand Canal, laden with every imaginable thing—from raw materials to finished goods—including furniture. Because efficiency of distribution and

Fig. 4. Xu Yang (active c. 1750–after 1776), *The Qianlong Emperor's Southern Inspection Tour*, scroll 6. Dated 1770. Handscroll, ink and color on silk. 68.8 cm × 1,994 cm. Metropolitan Museum of Art, New York, Purchase, The Dillion Fund Gift, 1988 (1988.350).

ease of transportation were important considerations to furniture makers and their clients, bulky pieces such as cabinets were often constructed so as to be easily dismantled, and joints and parts were marked to facilitate reassembly when they reached their point of arrival.

Design Traditions: From the *Lu Ban Jing* to the Early Qing Imperial Workshops

As noted above, the Ming-period carpenter's manual *Lu Ban Jing* is the earliest document that is presently known relative to furniture making. Along with calculations for the construction of building structures, agricultural implements, as well as for geomancy and sorcery, it contains pithy formulas for a wide range of popular furniture types. However, with its many incomplete entries, scanty measurements, and general lack of detail, it cannot be considered to be a practical reference manual.

An analysis of the measurements provided has indicated that these entries refer to relatively small-sized softwood furniture that predates the popularity of tropical hardwood furniture. The tables in the *Lu Ban Jing* are generally shorter—none greater than 75 cm in height—than the large body of extant hardwood tables, most of which exceed 80 cm. The garment rack, with a height of 150 cm and a width of 111 cm, is also rather small when compared to several extant examples with average dimensions of 170 cm (height) × 164 cm (width). Although the reader is warned many times that he must not deviate from the measurements, in several instances throughout the various entries, including the very first furniture entry, the reader is advised to "adjust the measurements of the piece in proportion to the size of the room."[34] The fact that the extant tropical hardwood furniture is generally 10 to 15 percent larger in its overall dimensions could indicate that these pieces were made for the large rooms and halls of wealthy families.

Because it is unlikely that craftsmen were sufficiently literate to read Lu Ban's Classic, it would appear that the general systems and details of furniture making were learned by observation and verbal instruction, as well as through the above-noted apprenticeships. Rather than being a practical carpenter's manual, the *Lu Ban Jing* was more probably a ritualistic manual, the very esoteric nature of which helped to maintain the long tradition found in building and furniture making.[35] Nevertheless, today the *Lu Ban Jing* clearly outlines the basic repertoire of Chinese furniture and provides a foundation block from which to understand the tradition of classical hardwood furniture.

Besides the rigid adherence to copying the work of a master, formulas for furniture design were likely passed from generation to generation through various means, including descriptive terminology and mnemonic rhymes. Numerous animated and colorful terms for carved furniture decoration are recorded in the *Lu Ban Jing*. Short, powerful "leopard legs" (*baojiao*) were commonly fit onto beds, stands, and low tables;[36] the term probably describes the short cabriole leg

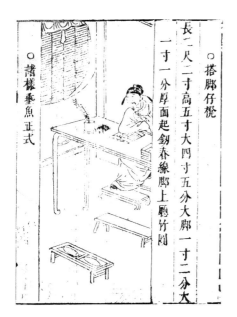

Fig. 5. Scholar at desk with footrests. Wanli reign period woodcut from the *Lu Ban Jing*.

(Klaas Ruitenbeek, *Carpentry and Building in Late Imperial China: A Study of the Fifteenth-century Carpenters' Manual Lu Ban Jing.* Leiden: E. J. Brill, 1993, p. 51)

known today. Examples may be seen in the cabriole legs of the bed in catalogue number 16 and the *kang* table in catalogue number 25. The shoulders of such legs were sometimes carved with "four-fanged swallowing heads" (*sichi tuntou;* cf. figs. 1 and 2);[37] and the feet were carved with "tiger claws" (*huzhao*).[38] Aprons were shaped with cusped and curvilinear designs "carved like water" (*sanwan leishui*),[39] or like a "praying mantis belly" (*tanglang du*),[40] as we see on the aprons of the incense stand in catalogue number 23. Other common forms of carved decoration included "paired hooks" (*shuanggou*)[41]—note the carvings on the splats and aprons of the round-back armchairs (cat. 11) and the front of the folding stool (cat. 2)—and "scrolled and intertwined lotus" (*shuanglian wan shuanggou*),[42] as on the aprons of the low-back chair (cat. 12) and the *kang* table (cat. 25). Such vivid, graphic concepts drawn from nature were easily transmitted orally and visually from one generation to the next, and they may also have inspired artisans to breathe life into their creations.

Several traditional memory rhymes used by woodcarvers have been gathered by the modern scholar Hu Wenyan. They convey standards for carving techniques and rules of general composition as well as pithy formulas for specific designs and their proportions. The composition of a dragon (cf. the carving of the folding stool, cat. 2, and of the terminals and standing spandrels of the garment rack, cat. 29) is represented by a few simple lines:

Deer horns, cow nose, and shrimp-like eyes,

fish scales, chicken claws, and body resembling a snake.

(*lujiao, niubi, xia yanjing*

yulin, jizhao, she si shen.)

And the proportions of the lion are described as:

Nine pounds of lion's body, ten pounds of head,

and one pound at the end of the tail.

(*jiu jin shishen, shi jin tou,*

yi jin weiba tuo houtou.)[43]

Memory rhymes were also probably used by carpenters to recall general layout and proportioning formulas.

Pattern books supplied standard designs and decorations in disciplines ranging from architecture to ink cakes, although no furniture pattern books have yet come to light. Woodcut illustrations achieved a high level of technical skill during the late Ming period and, to some extent, also preserved and popularized designs and forms. Popular illustrations were repeatedly copied as decorative imagery on porcelain, carved lacquer, and jade wares, as well as in inlay work. Furniture makers, too, may have turned to the woodcut illustrations added to the Wanli reign period edition of the *Lu Ban Jing* to recall patterns. The *huanghuali*, waisted, corner-leg table with "giant's arm braces" (cat. 20) could conceivably have been adapted from the furniture depicted in a woodcut illustration to the *Lu Ban Jing* (fig. 5), which shows a scholar reading at a table.

Much of the furniture maker's joinery terminology lacks clear origins, and many

63

terms are quite simplistic. For instance, the frequently recurring term *hejiao*[44] literally translates to "joined corner," without any respect to mechanics, when, in fact, most woodworking joints are joined corners. Using architectural terminology, Pu Songling makes an admirable attempt to describe how a screen panel fits into its base, but his description of the dovetail joinery that integrates the structure of a balance stand is more successful, in part because he uses the vivid woodworker's term, "interlaced fingers" (*chashou*).[45] Although early references to many specific terms have not yet been discovered, and perhaps were never recorded, Wang Shixiang's conversations with Beijing craftsmen have yielded some traditional terms that are still in use, such as *bawangcheng* (giant's arm brace). This interesting term retains its association with the famous third-century B.C. hero Xiang Yu, who used his arm to support heaven.[46]

Fig. 6. The cross-lapped giant's arm braces of cat. 20.

Xiang Yu's muscular strength underlies the *huanghuali* corner-leg table shown in catalogue number 20. This table exemplifies a work of classical Chinese art that, on first glance, may appear to be commonplace, but is, in fact, very profound. The thick aprons, generously sized frame members, and substantial understructure all reflect a time when regard for the consumption of materials was of secondary concern. Of greater importance to the single mind behind this masterpiece was the realization of classical proportions; the affected yet restrained animation; and the fully integrated construction. In its unity and mass, this table makes a significant contrast to the production pieces discussed above.

The table's integrated construction is exemplified in the unique crosslapped giant's arm braces at each end, as well as in the three-piece construction of the braces—which are joined with mortise-and-tenon joints to maximize the natural strength of the longitudinal woodgrain. These three-part braces, although rarely seen, are considerably stronger than S-shaped braces cut from single pieces of wood, which cannot avoid exposing the weak crossgrain.

Giant's arm braces appear to be derived from ancient architectural elements, for Han-period (206 B.C.–220 A.D.) tomb miniatures of towered buildings depict S-shaped corbel brackets supporting the roof overhangs.[47] Han tables were low, with short legs that did not require supports; they were simply tenoned into the paneled tops. As the mat-level culture was supplanted by the chair-level, however, braces on tables became necessary to support the longer legs. Wall murals and paintings from the Song and Yuan periods indicate that intermediate and floor stretchers were commonly fit between the legs of tables for reinforcement. As the use of chairs with such tables developed, C- and S-shaped braces (giant's arm braces) and high, humpback stretchers began to replace the awkward stretchers, which had interfered with the sitters' knees and legs. The robust system of bracing with giant's arm braces stabilized the legs, and also transferred some weight from the center of the table to the legs. Further developments in joinery leading up to the late-Ming period permitted furniture designs to become freer and more open, completely unencumbered by secondary stretchers. Nevertheless, the many examples of giant's arm braces attached with structurally weak (pinned) connections indicate that they continued to be used simply as a decorative device.

Furniture of restrained design had previously been associated with the cultivated class of scholars and high officials in China. The period following the lifting of the ban on maritime trade in 1567, however, was marked by a bustling economy with new-found wealth among the merchant class. Shortly thereafter, the rather sudden emergence of fine furniture of imported hardwoods was noted, as was its being considered fashionable by the lower classes: "Inside they would have good-quality wooden desks and a horse tail whisk for dusting the room they called their study, but what books they studied is open to question."[48]

This new socioeconomic climate, when the members of the heretofore disdained merchant class were attempting to surround themselves with the accouterments of those with codified rank and honor, stimulated guidebooks to tasteful living like Wen Zhenheng's *Zhang Wu Zhi* (Treatise on Superfluous Things, d. 1619). Descriptions of vulgar and elegant furnishings in precious woods like *huali, zitan, wumu,* and *tieli* are found therein. He detested the new sleek style of couch-bed, while praising the elegant antiquity of box-style platforms (*ta*) fit with rear and side railings.[49] Relative to wall tables he notes, "[their] raised ends (*qiaotou*)…must not be too sharp, but smooth and rounded." He goes on to praise those whose tops were figured with natural grain patterns, but detested those "carved with vulgar patterns such as dragons, phoenixes, flowers, and grasses."[50] Nonetheless, Wen's conservative attitudes were no match for the powerful, newly emerging forms and decorative styles that not only became the fashion of the time, but also embody the dynamic principles of classical Chinese furniture for the twentieth-century connoisseur.

The inept management and luxurious extravagance of the late-Ming rulers had left the imperial treasuries dry, and corruption led the period to its inevitable collapse. Ironically, the last Ming emperor's escape from political turmoil where he found sanctity in the realm of woodworking, also reflects the summit of classical Chinese furniture. Although there has been a tendency of late to associate the origins of hardwood furniture with lowly merchants and petty officials,[51] early eighteenth-century records from the Yongzheng imperial workshops indicate that the popularity of *huali, zitan,* and *hongdou* furniture was on par with that of lacquer furniture in the imperial court.

While the *Lu Ban Jing* predates the height of the classical period of furniture, which is generally considered to be centered around the seventeenth century, substantial archival notes from the Yongzheng reign period concerning furniture making in the imperial workshops, recently discussed by the scholar Zhu Jiajin, can be used to bracket the end of the era. These notes reveal what could be considered to be longstanding practices ranging from simply copying old designs to creating new designs to meet the whims and fancies of the emperor or court eunuchs. The copying of older traditional forms, either strictly or with subtle modifications, perpetuated the slow stylistic changes characteristic of the Chinese arts and has resulted in considerable difficulty in achieving the precise dating of

Chinese furniture. For instance, notes from the archives of the Yuanming Yuan, dated to the sixth year, third month, fourteenth day of Yongzheng's reign (1729), record that the official Hai Wang had requested new pieces of furniture—in lacquer as well as precious hardwoods—copied after older lacquer examples:

> According to the dimensions of the red lacquered table and the style of the black lacquered table, make one *zitan* table, one *hongdou* table, and four new red lacquered tables. Following the style of the red lacquered chair, make four *zitan* chairs and eight new red lacquer chairs. The placement as well as the [shapes of the] aprons and stretchers can be modified (*genggai*).[52]

During the early eighteenth century, many new styles and innovations in furniture design also emerged. The earliest evidence of hardwood furniture imitating that constructed from bamboo, either shaped realistically with nodules (cf. cat. 13) or abstractly realized with clean lines and rounded profiles, first begins to appear during this period, as we see in contemporary paintings and porcelain decoration. A large "bamboo style" (*zhushi*) stool with railings was produced in 1728 by Yongzheng imperial workshops after Hai Wang issued the edict: "Use *nanmu* or lacquered wood to make a "bamboo style" stool, length 2 *chi* 9 *cun*, width 2 *chi* 4 *cun*. At the back place a backrest with a height of 9 *cun*. The width of the two side pieces should be narrower by 2 to 3 *cun* (inches)."[53]

Many of the Yongzheng reign period documents concerning furniture making at the imperial workshops involve the multitalented official Hai Wang, who, in addition to acting as director of the board of works, was also instrumental in developing furniture designs. His instructions often request that models or drawings first be made for approval before actual objects were constructed:

> "Make one inlaid *huali chuang*, height 1 *chi* 1 *cun*, depth 4 *chi* 5 *cun*, length 7 *chi*." On the eighteenth day of the sixth month, a small model of the *chuang* (*hepai xiao chuang yang*) was submitted for approval. Afterward it was decreed: "Make it according to the model, but put two drawers in each of the two side rails." On the seventh month, fourteenth day [the full-sized piece] was made.[54]

> Yongzheng third year, eighth month, third day. The official Hai Wang issued the orders: "Make a pair of *huali* cabinets, height 2 *chi* 7 *cun*, width 1 *chi* 3 *cun*, length 4 *chi*. Fit the center shelf with a small drawer, and provide a large drawer on the lower shelf. Hang satin curtains on the outside. The drawers should be fitted with Western-style locks. Submit a drawing (*huayang*) for approval before making." On the ninth day of the eighth month, Hai Wang was shown four designs for the *huali* book cabinets and responded: "According to the design with the six drawers, make four *huali* book cabinets. According to the remaining three designs, make one each for a total of seven [cabinets]."[55]

Actually, drawings and miniature study models had both been used as architectural tools for the design of palaces, temples, and garden landscapes since at least the fifth century A.D.[56] The model furniture noted in these eighteenth-century records recalls the finely crafted, miniature wood furniture excavated from Ming tombs.

Perhaps these miniatures, too, reflected actual full-sized pieces that had been produced for the occupant of the tomb during his or her lifetime.

Reproducing one style in several different woods, or in softwoods with lacquer finishes, was another common practice.

> During the fourth year, on the twelfth day of the fifth month, the eunuch Wang An decreed: "Make a low throne chair for use on a boat." On the same day a model was made and submitted for approval, after which it was decreed: "The armrest does not need to be decorated; make it simple and rounded. The [panel of the] backrest should be a little higher and the seat should be soft." On the third day of the sixth month, the official Hai Wang presented a beautiful low throne chair made with a cushion as well as with a woven seat. It was furthermore decreed, "According to the measurements and style of this beautiful throne chair, additionally make two of *huali*, and two of *hongdou*."[57]

The pair of *zitan* round-back armchairs in this exhibition (cat. 11) is identical to two other pairs of *huanghuali* armchairs in private Hong Kong collections—further confirmation that identical designs were reproduced in different materials.[58]

Popular Hardwoods Used in Fine Furniture Making

The terminology for Chinese woods can be confusing, often without apparent links between ancient and modern times. Furthermore, the Chinese distinction between hardwood and softwood differs from that in the West. In China, the term *hardwood* refers to woods of the tropical variety, whose density, hardness, and imperviousness to boring insects qualify them as "hard." Softwoods are grouped into the category of *zamu,* literally "miscellaneous woods," which includes those woods whose deciduous nature characterizes them as hardwoods in Western botanical language.

The terms for specific woods are also somewhat generic, reflecting similar general characteristics of color, fragrance, hardness, and density rather than identification of species. After lifting the ban on maritime trade in 1567, Chinese cargo ships frequented ports in Southeast Asia, including the Spanish-controlled Philippines, where goods were traded for silver as well as for precious hardwoods. The purchasing pattern of these timber importers was noted by the nineteenth-century Spanish engineer, Domingo Vidal, whose observations likely reflect centuries-old practice and can shed some light on the confusion of terminology: "The Chinese never buy wood by invoice and attach little importance to names. Their methods of buying are very crude, the principal factors of importance to them are, that the wood does not float, and that it is of a dark color.... Their method of buying is by inspection, cutting the wood with an ax and examining it."[59]

As is apparent from the great number of extant examples, the tropical hardwood *huanghuali* appears to have been the most popular and widely used material for fine hardwood furniture production. The finest *huanghuali* has a translucent shimmering surface with abstract, figured patterns that delight the eye, its color ranging from reddish brown to golden yellow. The term *huanghuali* appears to be an early twentieth-century term coined to describe the patina of *huali* or *hualu*, as it was noted in premodern texts, whose mellowed, yellowish (*huang*) tone is the result of long exposure to light. Hainan Island is generally considered to be the main source of *huali*, although variations in the color, figure, and density of this fragrant wood suggests that several species from differing locations may exist.

Even more highly prized than *huanghuali* furniture was that of *zitan*. *Zitan* generally describes a wood that is extremely dense—to the point that it sinks in water—and laden with deep-red pigment that was used for dye. As early as the fourth and fifth centuries A.D., the use of a precious hardwood that sinks in water for the construction of beds is recorded.[60] The Jesuit priest Juan Jose Delgado, after arriving in Manila in 1711, also noted a similar Philippine hardwood called *tindalo*, which was highly prized by the Chinese:

> In China, where they say it [*tindalo*] sells for its weight in silver and is valued as such; they make from it many curious desks, chairs and stools. They also know how to preserve in the wood a blood-red color, washing it frequently in salt water. In time, if care is not taken, it changes to a dark color, but is very lustrous; it can be polished to such a degree that one's face can be seen in it.[61]

Early records indicate that the sources of *zitan* were mainly in Indochina, with some found in tropical forests of southern China.

Imperial workshop records from the Yongzheng and Qianlong reign periods indicate that supplies of *zitan* were becoming exhausted by the eighteenth century. Edicts were proclaimed forbidding its extravagant use[62] and alternative woods were recommended for various projects when the use of *zitan* was not fully justified: "Third year [1724], sixth month, eleventh day, in order to make a throne chair (*baozuo*) of *zitan* wood, Yi Chenwang memorialized the throne, after which it was decreed: 'It is not necessary to use *zitan* wood, make it from lacquer.'"[63]

The mixing of woods—in pieces such as *zitan* tables with *nanmu*-burl panels, or *huali* tables with *zitan* or *nanmu*-burl panels—which was also popular in Yongzheng's court, may also reflect the relative scarcity of both *zitan* and *nanmu* at that time. Many examples of *zitan* furniture from the Qianlong reign period and afterward are often constructed with reused or laminated materials.

Although today the mostly highly prized furniture making hardwoods are *huanghuali* and *zitan*, many other hardwoods were favored as well. The writings of Wen Zhenheng also indicate that *wumu* (ebony), *tielimu*, *nanmu*, and *huangyang* (boxwood) were considered to be tasteful furniture making woods in the late Ming period. According to references in the dictionary, *Cihai*, *hongdou* (red bean), which is frequently mentioned in the Yongzheng workshop notes along with other more familiar precious hardwoods, is another name for *xiangsi*, which, according to Wang Shixiang, is another term for *jichimu*.[64] In any case, finely crafted furniture produced from any of these beautiful woods appears to have been at least as highly valued as lacquer furniture.

Fig. 7. Square.

Fig. 9. Craftsmen making stools. Wanli reign period woodcut from the *Lu Ban Jing*.

(Klaas Ruitenbeek, *Carpentry and Building in Late Imperial China: A Study of the Fifteenth-century Carpenters' Manual Lu Ban Jing.* Leiden: E. J. Brill, 1993, p. 51)

Woodworking Tools

Whether he works from a drawing, a model, or an existing piece, the artisan transforms conceptions through his tools. Woodworkers in China generally had their own sets of tools, and from depictions in seventeenth-century woodcuts, including several illustrating the *Lu Ban Jing,* it is known that they were toted around from job to job in wicker baskets.[65] The invaluable Pu Songling wrote, "ax, chisel, *chan*, drill are all commonly used; square and inkline are passed down from the master."[66] As Pu indicates, layout and design tools were associated with the master's superior knowledge, but their use was also required of the carpenter.

Although earlier archaeological evidence indicates otherwise, Lu Ban, the legendary technical wizard of the Warring States period, is still credited with the invention of many carpentry tools, including the calibrated foot ruler (*chi*). One story that connects him to the length of the *chi* concerns the duke of Lu, who wanted to rebuild his palace on a grander scale but feared repercussions because of sumptuary regulations. The problem was solved, however, when Lu Ban simply created a longer foot rule for him.[67] The earliest foot rules (*chi*) found are from the Shang period and are approximately 15.8 centimeters in length, with decimal divisions of ten *cun* (inch), each of which is again divided into ten *fen*.[68] In fact, the length of the foot rule did increase from period to period, but by the Ming and Qing periods, the length of the carpenter's foot rule had stabilized at 30 centimeters. The carpenter's square (fig. 7) combines the foot rule with a right-angle leg and is used predominantly to mark out right angles for cutting boards to length or for laying out mortises and tenons.

The inkline (*modou*) was used to mark long, straight lines on planks of wood to serve as guides for sawing and planing straight edges, and its inkwell provided a source of ink for the bamboo brushes that were also used to mark pieces of wood. An early tradition of artistically carved inklines is evidenced in the late Ming encyclopedia, *San Cai Tu Hui,* where a bird-shaped example is illustrated.[69] Inklines were carved and decorated in various fashions, sometimes resembling shoes and other times, as in the example in this exhibition (fig. 8), with an animal head from which the string itself emerges. The inkline is fit with a reel at the center similar to that used for fishing, and one end is hollowed out to form the inkpot. The inkwell was filled with a wadding of silk waste or moxa saturated with black ink.[70] Having been pulled through the reservoir of saturated material, the freshly inked line is stretched taut between two points on the flat surface of a board and snapped upward from the midpoint, leaving an impression of the straight line marked on the board. The end of the inkline is often attached to a small wooden block fit with a sharp iron pin, which could be pressed into the wood so that the lines could be marked by one person. Legend has it that Lu Ban also invented this device—to avoid inconveniencing his wife when he needed someone to hold the end of the line. This, as well as the workbench stop—a small block attached to the bench to prevent a workpiece from slipping while planing—are now both termed "Lu Ban's wife" (*Lu Ban qi*).[71]

Both compass and square are depicted on a Han tomb pillar as traditional emblems of Fuxi and Nugua, mythological gods who brought order to chaos.[72] Because the circle and the square came to symbolize *tian* (heaven) and *di* (earth), respectively, the tools used to make these forms also acquired cosmic associations. Their relationships are clarified in a passage in which Lu Ban explains the need to transmit his accumulated knowledge and observations to short-sighted mortals:

> Roundness not brought about by use of compasses, squareness not brought about by use of the square, such is the natural shape of Heaven and Earth. Using compasses to bring about roundness, using the square to bring about squareness, such is truly the faculty of man's senses with regard to these shapes.[73]

Fig. 10. Two-handled push plane.

General carpentry and furniture making tools are depicted in the illustrations to the *Lu Ban Jing*. A workshop scene filled with stools and benches (fig. 9) depicts a superintendent watching as a craftsman surfaces a bench top with a traditional two-handled "push plane" (*tuibao*), sometimes called a "bird [wing] plane" (*wu bao*) after its wing-shaped handles (see fig. 10). A scraper plane, or literally "centipede plane" (*wugong bao*), used to produce a highly polished surface, lies beneath the other completed bench. The mallet and chisel were instrumental in cutting mortises and shaping tightly fitting tenons. A bow drill is also depicted in this illustration. It was used to bore small holes into which pins were driven to secure the mortise to the tenon, as well as to drill the holes around the inside perimeter of the seat frame through which the soft cane seats were woven.

Fig. 11. Molding plane.

The plane was developed relatively late in the history of Chinese woodworking tools. It is now generally considered to have appeared some time before the middle of the Ming period.[74] Previously, paring tools were skillfully worked to refine roughly adzed surfaces. Such a tool was the long, spade-shaped, knifing tool called *chan*, illustrated in the fifteenth-century children's primer *Xinbian duixiang*.[75] Although evidently still in use during the middle Ming period, these paring tools were eventually replaced by various types of planes that removed thin layers of wood much more quickly and with considerably more precision.

Fig. 12. "Centipede" or scraper plane.

Although we cannot yet establish at what point the plane came into common use, it is remarkable to consider the many surviving wooden artifacts, not to mention the sophisticated technique of producing pieced columns, as illustrated in the Song *Yingzao fashi*,[76] all of which were realized without it. Perhaps it was an esoteric tool kept secret by members of the cult of Lu Ban, for the first firmly dated depictions of planes are those in the illustrated Wanli edition of the *Lu Ban Jing*.[77] At least two types of planes are illustrated: the common scrub plane, used to flatten the surfaces of short pieces, and the jointing plane, used to plane longer surfaces straight. The first detailed descriptions of the plane appear in compendiums and dictionaries compiled after the sixteenth century. An entry in the 1609 technological treatise *Tiangong Kaiwu* (The Exploitation of Works of Nature) is unusually specific:

Fig. 13. Shoulder plane.

Fig. 14. Back saw.

Fig. 15. Frame saw.

[The blade of] the common plane is made sharp with one-inch steel laminated onto its cutting iron. It protrudes the smallest fraction at an angle from the opening of the [lower] surface, and therefore [is used to] smooth flat the surface of wood. [This process] was called leveling (*zhun*) by the ancients. Long ones can be supported [upside-down] to lay level with the blade exposed. Wood can then be planed by pulling [or pushing over the cutting edge]. This is called a "push plane" (*tui bao*). Barrel makers often use it. The common type has two winglike wooden handles perpendicular to the body for pushing [the plane] forward. Used for fine woodworking is the molding plane (*qixian bao*), with a plane blade about two *fen* in width. That for scraping wood extremely smooth is called a "centipede plane" (*wugong bao*). Ten or more small knives are clinched within a wooden handle and look like centipede legs.[78]

Twenty years later, additional details appear in the *Zheng zi tong*, a dictionary of characters, where the plane is also linked to its predecessor, the *chan*:

Plane (*bao*), tool for straightening wood. The iron blade is shaped like a *chan* and is held tightly within a wooden block so that it cannot move. The wooden block has an opening, and at the sides are two small handles with which the hands can repeatedly push it. Wood shavings come out through the opening. It is faster to use than the *chan*.[79]

The Japanese *Wakan sansaizu-e* (Chinese and Japanese Universal Encyclopedia), published in 1712, also compares this relatively new tool to the handheld paring knives:

The ancients used a spearlike planing knife (Chinese *qiangsi*), but commonly used for more than one hundred years is the *tsuki-ganna* [push plane]. Although the two forms are different, they achieved similar results. Compared to the planing knife, it is much faster to use and more precise, however, and today is commonly written as *bao*.[80]

These references indicate that the quick and accurate *bao* evolved from the early planing knives and the spokeshave plane, and that it was not known in Japan before the sixteenth century, when the push-plane was introduced from China. Although later Japanese woodworking tools are renowned for their excellent laminated-steel blades, it is clear from various passages in the *Tiangong Kaiwu* that Chinese ironsmiths of the late Ming period were still well versed in the art of producing high-quality blades with steel forge-welded onto cutting edges. The dependence of carpenters on ironsmiths is made clear in Pu Songling's lines, "Ax and adze handles are cut and shaped by themselves, but plane blade, gouge, and saw [blade] all cost them money."[81]

Molding planes facilitated the shaping of various decorative profiles (fig. 11). The knife blades of molding planes are cut with a skewed profile of the desired molding section, to which the sole of the wooden body is shaped to match. With each repeated run of the molding plane over the board's length, paper-thin cuttings are shaved from the surface until the razor-sharp cutting edge cuts its full profile. The molding plane, or perhaps beading plane cited above in the reference from *Tiangong Kaiwu*, with width of two *fen* (approximately six millimeters), may directly relate to the "two-*fen* [wide] beading" (*er fen xian*) plane specified for the legs of an Eight Immortal's table in the *Lu Ban Jing*.[82] Wide beaded moldings of similar dimension are found on several pieces in this exhibition (cf. cat. 27 and 29). Other moldings recorded in the *Lu Ban Jing,* such as *jianji xian* (sword-ridge molding), *mahuang xian* (string molding), *qipan xian* (chessboard molding), *yanzhu xian* (bamboo molding), and *wandi xian* (bowl-bottom molding) also suggest a variety of simple profiles that were shaped with different molding planes.[83]

Because these planes were generally custom-made for workshops, and continued to be used from generation to generation, the study and identification of molding profiles offers a method of identifying the work of the specific workshops. The earliest profiles seem to be relatively simple, rounded shapes, or with ogival or *cyma reversa* curves (also called "ice-plate moldings" by modern Beijing craftsmen[84]), and are commonly found on tabletops and beds; large concave moldings, often with a step, were common to the seat frames of chairs and stools. As plane technology developed, the variety of moldings and beadings increased, as did their levels of intricacy and refinement.

The "centipede plane" (fig. 12) cited above from *Tiangong Kaiwu* is of particular interest relative to the production of furniture from tropical hardwoods like *huanghuali* and *zitan,* which have interlocked grain and are prone to tearing out regardless of the direction from which they are planed. A scraper can shave finely the surface of "difficult-to-work" woods without tearing out the contrary grain. These planes are still used by modern *hongmu* furniture makers and restorers in China. Two Americans who made a woodworking tour through China during the late 1980s took special note of this uniquely Chinese tool, which was previously unknown to them. In an article in *Fine Woodworking*, they reported that scraper planes were available in Shanghai marketplaces, but the best ones were made by the workmen themselves, utilizing short pieces of old saw blades:

> The blades are held in place on the tool by compression alone. The stock is kerfed using a handsaw with all the set removed, which makes the kerf an exact match for the thickness of the steel. The extended projections of the short grain between the kerfs are flexible enough to allow all the blades to slip into place, except for the last one. This one must be forced in, and this process tightens up the entire row. After mounting, the blades are filed into perfect alignment, and the back side of each cutting edge is beveled to about 60 degrees.[85]

In order to use material efficiently, large, flat elements of Chinese furniture are typically constructed with a thin panel housed within a framework of more substantial dimension; today this technique is termed "frame-and-panel construction." The thin outside edge of the panel floats within a groove cut along the inside of the frame, and is locked in place by the mitered frame, which is joined with mortise-and-tenon joints. These tongue-and-groove joints were produced with rebate and grooving planes. The rebate, or shoulder, plane (fig. 13) is configured to shave a notch along the edge of a board or panel; the width of this notch is held constant by the integrated guiding edge of the sole plate. Most panels have a notched shoulder on the front side; however, because handcrafted panels were not generally of uniform thickness, they were beveled along a scribed line on the rear side with a jack, or common, plane, to leave a tongue of uniform width. Grooving planes, or "plough planes," were, as the name suggests, used to cut narrow grooves into frame members.

The use of small back saws can be dated to the Warring States period. Five small back saws as well as a number of other beautifully crafted bronze woodworking tools were found in a tomb considered to be that of the king of Bashu (an ancient kingdom in modern Sichuan province). Each of the back saws has a bronze blade set into the groove of a long wooden handle and secured with lacquered caning.[86] Although these early saws relate closely to the modern Chinese *jiabei ju* (clinched back saw), they were only useful in cutting relatively thin material across the grain. With the development of iron blades, however, back saws (fig. 14) became instrumental in the precise cutting of complex tenon and dovetail joinery. In the early part of this century, Hommel noted that these saws were indispensable to the production of high-quality furniture. Like the traditional Japanese saw, these saws all have the teeth oriented to cut on the pull stroke rather than the push stroke.[87]

The H-shaped frame saw (fig. 15), which holds a long narrow blade in tension, first appeared in China sometime after the Tang period (618–906) and was possibly introduced from the West, along the Silk Road. Previously timbers were split roughly with wedges, and boards were hewn with adzes. Timber shortages prompted more efficient use of material during the Song period, and during this time lighter architectural forms appeared, along with more sophisticated joinery. Early references to the frame saw are found in the Song-period *Yingzao fashi,* as well as in the Song painting, *Spring Festival on the River,* in which a scene of cartwrights at work depicts a handsaw lying on the ground.[88] The deeply cut teeth on a two-man ripping saw are often oriented in both directions to equalize each sawyer's exertion. The shorter frame-saw blade, patterned with finer teeth, all oriented in one direction, was a utility saw for woodworkers, and was generally used to cut boards to length across the grain. Hommel noted that the early twentieth-century saws were made of hardwood in a variety of sizes, and that the saw blade was usually set at a slight angle to the plane of the frame, so that the carpenter could guide it along the desired line.[89]

The study of woodworking tools renews our respect and admiration for the early master furniture makers, who painstakingly handcrafted each element of chair, table, or cabinet from the raw material. An understanding of handtools and their particular traces is also crucial in any attempt to distinguish period Chinese furniture from those heavily restored or fraudulent pieces produced with modern tools.

This brief foray into the world of the woodworker has only touched upon a many-faceted realm that awaits further investigation into yet-undiscovered sources. Here, within Lu Ban's domain, lies the sphere of furniture makers who catered to the needs of a widely diverse society, such needs ranging from commonplace furnishings to dowry furniture richly decorated with auspicious wishes for the newlyweds; from simple, elegant furnishings made in accordance with traditional tastes and the specialized demands of the gentry to smart, stylish furniture for the nouveau riche; and finally to objects that were skillfully crafted to satisfy the whims of court eunuchs and emperors. Although individual craftsmen of furniture remained anonymous, their artistic spirit radiates from many of the works that have survived to this time. Combined with the wisdom of Lu Ban, precious raw materials were ingeniously shaped with tools resulting in one of the world's greatest furniture making traditions.

Notes

1. "Master Ch'ing cut wood to make a bell frame. When completed, it greatly startled the viewers, who thought that it must have been the work of spirits. Duke of Lu, on seeing it asked, 'With what technical skill did you make it?' He answered, 'I am just a workman; there is no technical skill to speak of. However, I have one thing to say. When I was about to make the frame, I had never dared to waste my *ch'i*. I would fast to calm my heart. For the first three days of fasting, I never let the thought of happy occasions, rewards, rank, or emolument enter my mind. During the five days of fasting, I never thought of any criticism, whether condemning or approving and whether well done in the execution of my work or poorly done. In the seven days of fasting, I quietly became unaware of my four limbs and my body. During that period neither the public nor the court was in my thought. My attention was so completely concentrated on my work that nothing outside disturbed me. Then I went into the woods looking for material which would fit my scheme naturally. When I saw the form of the bell frame in the wood, I proceeded to have the frame made. Otherwise, I would stay my hand. Mine was to blend nature with nature. This may be the reason why people thought the frame was the work of a divine spirit.'" (Quoted from Vincent Yu-chuang Shih, *The Literary Mind and the Carving of Dragons*. Hong Kong: Chinese University Press, 1983, p. xxiii.)

2. Both compass and square became the traditional emblems of Fuxi and Nugua, mythological gods who brought order to chaos. As the circle and the square came to symbolize *tianyuan* (round heaven) and *difang* (square earth) respectively, the tools used to make these forms also acquired cosmic associations. The *San Cai Tu Hui* credits two Warring States–period philosophers, Mengzi and Zhuangzi, with a role in the development of the saw; the latter described its newly unleashed potential as the external manifestation of *li* (eternal principles). (Wang Ji, *San Cai Tu Hui* (Pictorial Encyclopedia of Heaven, Earth, and Man), 1609. 3 vols. Shanghai: Shanghai Guji Chubanshe, 1985, p. 1298.)

3. Zhang Yinwu, "Chu-Style Furniture." *Journal of the Classical Chinese Furniture Society* 4:3 (Summer 1994), p. 55; Lou Yudong, ed., *Xinyang Chumu.* Beijing: Wenwu Press, 1986, p. 64; and Sichuan sheng bowuguan/Xindu xian wenwu guanlisuo (Sichuan Museum, Xindu Cultural Administration Office), "Sichuan Xindu Changuo muguomu" (A Warring States Wooden Coffin Excavated in Xindu, Sichuan). *Wenwu* 1981:6, p. 10.

4. Curtis Evarts, "From Ornate to Unadorned: A Study of a Group of Yokeback Chairs." *Journal of the Classical Chinese Furniture Society* 3:2 (Spring 1993), p. 28.

5. See Curtis Evarts, "The Development of the Waisted Form and Variations in Its Joinery." *Journal of the Classical Chinese Furniture Society* 1:3 (Summer 1991), pp. 38–47.

6. Klaas Ruitenbeek, *Carpentry and Building in Late Imperial China: A Study of the Fifteenth-century Carpenters' Manual Lu Ban Jing.* Leiden: E. J. Brill, 1993, p. 15

7. Ibid., p. 19.

8. Eugene Cooper, *The Wood-carvers of Hong Kong: Craft Production in the World Capitalist Periphery.* Cambridge, Eng.: Cambridge University Press, 1980, p. 23.

9. Ibid., pp. 23–28.

10. Ruitenbeek, p. 129.

11. Ibid., p. 154.

12. Chen Shiqi, *Mingdai de gongjiang zhidu* (Craftsmen Regulations of the Ming Period). *Lishi Yanjiu* 6 (1955), pp. 61–88.

13. Zhu Jiajin, "Yongzheng nian de jiaju zhizao kao" (A Study of the Yongzheng Imperial Furniture Workshops, Part 1). *Gugong bowuyuan yuankan* 1985:3, p. 106.

14. Cooper, p. 132.

15. This was conveyed to this author by Ben F. Schaberg, Jr., in spring 1995, during his visit to the Museum of Classical Chinese Furniture at Renaissance, California.

16. Rudolf P. Hommel, *China at Work.* Cambridge, Mass. and London: M.I.T. Press, 1969, pp. 224–29.

17. *Quercus serrata*

18. *Yu* is listed twice, both as a hardwood and as a softwood.

19. Translation after Li Mingzhong, *Yingzao fashi* (Architectural Methods). Beijing: Zhongguo Shudian, 1989, *juan* 24, p. 8.

20. Translation after *Pu Songling ji* (Collected Works of Pu Songling). Beijing: Zhonghua Shuju Chuban, 1962, pp. 742–43.

21. Tan Junping. *Mudiao Gongyi* (The Art of Wood Carving). Beijing: Zhongguo Linye Chubanshe, 1992, pp. 76–87.

22. Cooper, p. 35.

23. Translation after *Pu Songling ji*, pp. 742–43.

24. Mette Siggstedt, "Chinese Root Furniture." *The Museum of Far Eastern Antiquites Bulletin,* no. 63 (1991), p. 149.

25. Cf. plates 6, 7, and 8 in Maurice Dupont, *Les Meubles de la Chine*. Paris: Librairie des Arts Décoratifs, 1959.

26. Curtis Evarts, "Classical Chinese Furniture in the Piccus Collection." *Journal of the Classical Chinese Furniture Society* 2:4 (Autumn 1992), p. 16; Evarts, "From Ornate to Unadorned," pp. 24–33; and Curtis Evarts, "Best of the Best: An Exhibition of Ming Furniture from Private Collections." *Arts of Asia*, May–June 1995, p. 135.

27. Wang Shixiang, *Classic Chinese Furniture: Ming and Early Qing Dynasties*. Trans. by Sarah Handler and the author. Hong Kong: Joint Publishing Co., 1986, p. 91.

28. Chen Zengbi, ed., *Zhongyang gongyi meishu xueyuan yuancang zhenpin tulu, di er ji, mingshi jiaju* (Treasures from the Collection of the Central Academy of Arts. Vol. 2: Ming-style Furniture). Xianggang: Jieyijia chuban gongsi chuban, 1994. p. 24.

29. Nigel Cameron, *Classic Chinese Furniture: The Ming Tradition*. Exhibition catalogue. Hong Kong: Hong Kong Land Co., 1992, cover.

30. Sarah Handler, "A Little World Made Cunningly: The Chinese Canopy Bed." *Journal of the Classical Chinese Furniture Society* 2:2 (Spring 1992), fig. 16.

31. Wang Shixiang, *Classic Chinese Furniture*, p. 191.

32. Exhibited at the China Arts and Crafts Museum, Beijing, Nov. 11–13, 1991. For description see Curtis Evarts, "A Report on the First International Symposium of Chinese Ming Domestic Furniture." *Journal of the Classical Chinese Furniture Society*, vol. 2, no. 1. (Rev. ed.) Renaissance, Cal.: Classical Chinese Furniture Society, 1992.

33. Although it falls outside the scope of this article, it should be noted that most of the mid- to late-eighteenth-century furniture depicted in the painting would today be considered "Ming-style" furniture.

34. Ruitenbeek, p., 31.

35. See Curtis Evarts, "The Classic of Lu Ban and Classical Chinese Furniture" (*Journal of the Classical Chinese Furniture Society* 3:1 (Winter 1993)) for an analysis of the furniture entries in the *Lu Ban Jing* alongside the extant examples of hardwood furniture.

36. Ruitenbeek, pp. 49, 72, 73, 74, and 75.

37. Ibid., p. 46.

38. Ibid., pp. 53 and 66.

39. Ibid., pp. 31, 44, 45, 47, 48, 63, and 73.

40. Ibid., p. 74.

41. Ibid., pp. 49 and 64.

42. Ibid., p. 74.

43. Translation after Hu Wenyan, "Mingshi jiaju de zhuangshi" (The Decoration of Ming-style Furniture). *Gugong bowuyuan yuankan*, 1985.1, p. 82.

44. Ruitenbeek, pp. 37, 66, 73, and 77.

45. *Pu Songling ji*, p. 743.

46. Wang Shixiang, *Classic Chinese Furniture,* p. 312.

47. Joseph Needham, *Science and Civilisation in China*. Vol. IV: *Physics and Physical Technology*. Part III: *Civil Engineering and Nautics*. Taipei: Caves Books, 1985, p. 126.

48. Wang Shixiang, *Connoisseurship of Chinese Furniture*. 2 vols. Hong Kong: Joint Publishing Co., 1990, p. 17.

49. Wen Zhenheng, *Zhangwu zhi* (Treatise on Superfluous Things). Compiled 1615–20. *Yishu congbian* 29.357, *juan* 6, pp. 1a and 1b.

50. Ibid., pp. 2a and 2b.

51. Craig Clunas, "Chinese Furniture and Western Designers." *Journal of the Classical Chinese Furniture Society*, vol. 3, no. 1, 1992, p. 69.

52. Translation after Zhu, "Yongzheng nian de jiaju zhizao kao," p. 107

53. Ibid., p. 110.

54. Translation after Zhu Jiajin, "Yongzheng nian de jiaju zhizao kao (xu)" (A Study of the Yongzheng Imperial Furniture Workshops, Part 2). *Gugong bowuyuan yuankan* 1985:4, p. 80.

55. Ibid, p. 81.

56. Needham, p. 105

57. Zhu, "Yongzheng nian de jiaju zhizao kao," p. 110.

58. Two identical pairs of chairs made of *huanghuali* were noted and photographed by this author in Hong Kong in 1992.

59. Vidal goes on to mention the Philippine woods that the Chinese preferred, including those of Narra, Tindalo, and Camagon, which were well known at that time for their use in fine furniture making. (Captian George P. Ahern, *Compilation of Notes on the Most Important Timber Tree Species of the Philippine Islands*. Manila: Forestry Bureau, 1901, p. 97.)

60. *Shiyi ji* (Memoirs on Neglected Matters), and *Yiyuan* (Garden of Strange Things), in *Cui Rongxue. Zhongguo jiaju shi—zuoju bian* (The History of Chinese Furniture: Seating Furniture). Taipei: Ming Wen shuju, 1987, p. 61.

61. Ahern, pp. 81–82.

62. Zhu, "Yongzheng nian de jiaju zhizao kao (xu)," p. 85.

63. Translation after Zhu, "Yongzheng nian de jiaju zhizao kao," p. 110.

64. Wang Shixiang, *Connoisseurship of Chinese Furniture,* p. 187; and *Cihai* (Dictionary). Hong Kong: Zhonghua Shuju Yinxing, 1992, p. 1030. Although Zhu Jiajin suggests that *hongdou* might be the same as *hongmu* (Zhu, "Yongzheng nian de jiaju zhizao kao," p. 106), more evidence will be required at this point to support his conjecture.

65. Cf. Fu Xihua, *Zhongguo Gudian Wenxue Banhua Xuanji* (Selected Woodblock Illustrations to Classic Chinese Literature). 2 vols., Shanghai, 1981, p. 669; *Mingdai banhua yishu tushi tezhan zhuanji* (Exhibition of Graphic Art in Printed Books of the Ming Dynasty: Selected Exhibits). Taipei: National Central Library, 1989, p. 151; and Ruiteenbeek *juan* I, pp. 16a, 17a, 29b, and 32a.

66. *Pu Songling ji*, p. 742.

67. Ruitenbeek, p. 92.

68. Zhang Shengfu, ed., *Zhongguo gudai duliangheng tuji* (Weights and Measures in China through the Ages). Beijing: Wenwu Chubanshe Chuban, 1984, p. 2.

69. Cf. Wang Ji, p. 1111.

70. Hommel, p. 250.

71. Cooper, p. 123.

72. Anthony Christie, *Chinese Mythology*. New York: Peter Bedrick Books, 1987, pp. 88–89.

73. Ruitenbeek, p. 153.

74. Sun Zi, "Woguo gudai de pingmu gongju" (Ancient Chinese Wood-surfacing Tools). *Wenwu* 1987:10, p. 75.

75. L. Carrington Goodrich, *Hsin-pien tui-xiang szu-yen* (Fifteenth-century Illustrated Chinese Primer). Facsimile reproduction with introduction and notes. Hong Kong: Hong Kong University Press, 1967, p. 6.

76. Li, *juan* 30, pp. 18a and 18b.

77. Ruitenbeek, pp. 22, 24, and 30.

78. Translation after Song Yingxing, *Tiangong Kaiwu* (The Exploitation of Works of Nature). Zhongguo gudai ban-hua congkan (*Collection of Ancient Chinese Woodblock Print Publications*), vol. 3 of 4. Shanghai: Shanghai Guji Chubanshe, 1988, p. 899.

79. Translation after Sun, p. 74.

80. Translation after William H. Coaldrake, *The Way of the Carpenter: Tools and Japanese Architecture*. New York: Weatherhill, 1990, p. 147.

81. *Pu Songling ji*, p. 742.

82. Ruitenbeek, p. 234.

83. Ibid., pp. 341–42.

84. Wang Shixiang, *Classic Chinese Furniture,* p. 39.

85. John Kreigshauser and Nancy Lindquist, "Woodworkers' Tour of China: Ancient Ways Persist in the Age of Automation." *Fine Woodworking* no. 74 (Jan.–Feb. 1989), p. 83.

86. Sichuan sheng bowuguan, p. 10.

87. Hommel, pp. 238–39.

88. Gugong bowuyuan canghuaji bianji weiyuan gong bian. *Zhongguo lidai huihua: Gugong bowuyuan canghuaji*. Vol. II *Song Daibufen 1* (The History of Chinese Painting: Palace Museum Painting Collection. Vol. 2: Song Period, Part 1). Beijing: Renmin Meishi Chubanshe, 1981, p. 73.

89. Hommel, p. 228.

Fig. 1. Model bedroom furniture from the tomb of Pan Yunzheng. Shanghai Museum, Shanghai.

Conjectures on Models of Ming-Period Furniture Excavated from the Pan Yunzheng Tomb in Shanghai

Wang Zhengshu

Furniture is an indispensable daily necessity in civilized human society. As early as the Tang–Song period (618–1279) of Chinese history, mankind's evolution from squatting on mats to sitting upright laid the basis for the development of furniture, the dimensions of which correspond to human proportions. By the Ming period (1368–1644), furniture was not only available in great variety, but was also finely crafted, scientifically designed, and made from high-quality material, mainly hardwood. Thus the art of Ming-period furniture has become an important part of the Chinese cultural heritage. The only drawback is that wood is hard to preserve and, to date, little if any furniture from before the middle Ming period is extant. Even furniture from the late Ming period, although preserved intact, is hard to date with any precision. Thus, one important way to enlarge our knowledge of, and upgrade our skill in, identifying and dating Ming furniture is through the study of the furniture models that have been excavated.

For many years now, the dozens of models of Ming furniture excavated from six tombs in the Shanghai area, especially the wooden examples from the tomb of Pan Yunzheng, have provided important material clues to the study of the shape, structure, and ornamentation of Ming furniture. Most of the available examples of model furniture that were used as burial objects were made of clay, rarely of wood. The disadvantage of clay models is that the outlines tend to be indistinct and the joinery cannot be displayed. Thus the study of Ming furniture must rely on wooden models, such as those from the tomb of Pan Yunzheng.

Pan Yunzheng was born during the reign of the Emperor Jiajing (1522–66) and died in the reign of the Emperor Wanli (1573–1620). During his lifetime, he had been an official of the eighth rank, supervisor of Guanglu monastery. In August 1960, his tomb was unearthed in Zhaojiabang Road in Shanghai. The furniture pieces, which constituted only part of the burial objects, were made of the local *ju* wood and were constructed on a reduced scale with proper proportions. Included among the wooden furnishings in his tomb and that of his son were a bed, a daybed, cabinets, tables, chairs, a garment rack, a chamber pot, and many other household necessities. Individually and as a group, these objects provide a wealth of information for the study of Ming furniture.

Alcove Bed

Due to its bulk and complex design, the model alcove bed (*babu chuang*; cat. 30a) in the Pan Yunzheng tomb is rare among archaelogical finds. To date, only two alcove-bed models have been excavated. One is the burial object of Wang Xijue of the Ming, which was unearthed in Suzhou; the other is the model excavated from the Pan family tomb in Shanghai. Of these two, the Pan model is made according to proportional measurements on a miniature scale, and thus provides a rare standard object for study. Especially worthy of note is the bed's wooden bottom, which lies close to the floor and therefore could have rotted easily. Obviously it would be unlikely for this kind of bed to be preserved intact after several centuries of use. Therefore, apart from clues garnered from Ming-period books, ancient burial objects are our most important source for the study of the alcove bed.

The Pan alcove bed is structured after a frame bed composed of six pillars with encircling rails and a covered entrance. Its main features are a floor board and four posts at the front of the bed. The spaces between the posts are fenced together in a manner that is similar to the covered verandas built onto houses in ancient times. The front alcove space thus created is small, yet it is still possible to carry on some activities within its confines. In the Ming period, it was customary to put a footstool in front of the bed, with a seat installed at one end of the alcove and a desk and lamp at the other, thus creating an environment of great comfort. The Ming book on carpentry—the *Lu Ban Jing*—referred to alcove beds as "cool beds," emphasizing the features of comfort and relaxation.

No records of the alcove-bed form from before the Ming period are known. Judging from existing archaeological finds and historical records, it appeared only in the late Ming period and was owned solely by members of the upper class. For a study of its evolution, one must look for hints from a pottery bed stored in the Shanghai Museum and the alcove bed of Wang Xijue excavated in Suzhou.

The pottery bed at the Shanghai Museum has all the functions of a bed, but is modeled on the architecture of ancient halls, which may be seen in three of its aspects:

(1) The four posters at the front of the bed create a corridor space. The top of the posts are ornamented with *dougong* brackets, while the bottom is fitted into a drum-shaped stone base. This is a familiar aspect of the facade of ancient buildings, which typically contained three rooms. Behind the four posters, the bed itself resembles an inner room.

(2) The structure of the bottom of the bed is modeled on a pedestal base, typical of ancient architecture. The waist of ancient Chinese furniture evolved from this type of base.

(3) The upper part of the bed is ringed by wooden latticework, which is an adaptation from the window design of ancient architecture.

The structure of this pottery bed makes it apparent that it was designed in full accordance with the layout of ancient buildings. The corridor in front of the bed was precisely the prevalent form for the Ming alcove bed. The example preserved in the Suzhou Museum is basically the same as that preserved in Shanghai; particularly worthy of note are the stone bases of the four posts, which are similar to those of the pottery bed. By the time the alcove bed in Pan's tomb in Shanghai was designed, the stone bases of the posts had disappeared, which suggests that this could be considered to be a distinct feature of the alcove bed of the late Ming period.

Cabinets

The cabinet is a basic type of Ming furniture. Many examples have been handed down, but few can be dated accurately. Thus, for a study of Ming cabinets, burial objects among dated archaeological finds can be of great assistance.

Chinese cabinets are defined primarily by rounded or angular corners. As far as this writer is aware, all cabinet models found among excavated burial objects have been round-cornered, and most are made of clay. Only the four excavated in Shanghai are wood. Two of these are from the Pan tomb (cat. 30c), while two others are from the Yan tomb at Zhongshanbei Road, both being works from the Wanli reign period. The four cabinets unearthed in Shanghai offer us the following clues:

(1) Round-cornered cupboards have doors on vertical wooden post hinges (*li zhu*), while square-cornered cupboards have doors on metal hinges. To judge from the make and tightness of the doors, the square-cornered cupboards are of more complex design and shut more tightly, making them the superior form of cabinet. The four cabinets excavated in Shanghai come from two different tomb sites; all have doors on vertical wooden-post hinges and not metal hinges. This writer's opinion is that the round-cornered cabinet, which is the product of the traditional carpentry art of the times, predates the square-cornered cabinet. These four model cabinets were all buried in tombs belonging to people who were members of the political and economic elite. Yan was a member of the local gentry, while Pan had been a member of a notable family in Shanghai. The fact that they used round-cornered cabinets for burial objects indicates that that such cabinets must have been fashionable during the late Ming.

(2) Of the four cabinets excavated in Shanghai, only one had straight legs; all the others had splayed legs. Since cabinets are standing pieces of furniture that must bear a substantial amount of weight, the use of splayed legs makes them more stable. Of all the unearthed furniture objects, the majority have splayed legs, which demonstrates one of the typical characteristics of Ming furniture.

(3) The cabinets unearthed at the Pan tomb were made on a miniature scale, but were not fitted with interior drawers, which was also the case for the two cabinets unearthed from the Yan tomb. They were all fitted with a shelf that divides the interior into two sections. Although simple, this approach provides for a neat design that is in keeping with the characteristics of Ming furniture.

Chairs

No dated southern official's hat armchair has been preserved for posterity. But two such chairs were found among the burial objects in the Pan Yunzheng tomb (see cat. 30i) and two others were among the finds in the Pan Hui tombs. The two chairs excavated from the Pan Hui tomb were ugly and crudely made, but evidently belonged to the same era and locality and were constructed according to the same design as those from the Pan Yunzheng tomb. The four chairs share several features, all of which were derived from the style of the era:

(1) All four southern official's hat armchairs have the bow-shaped headrest.

(2) In the design of the fittings for all four chairs, the pipe-join, mortise-and-tenon

method of joinery was used to attach the headrest to the vertical post, and the front post to the arm. This method of joinery consists of one piece furnished with a tenon that fits into a mortise on the other.

(3) These chairs all have legs that splay slightly outward, while the vertical posts of the chair as well as the front post bend inward, thereby achieving a certain stability.

(4) The legs of each chair were adorned with aprons, mainly with a plain or cusped outline; the curvilinear, "belly" outline type is not seen.

(5) Song- and Yuan-period armchairs and side chairs were all fitted with stretchers between the legs that were raised high above the ground. Those of the Ming period were rather low and the stretchers on the two sides usually were higher than those on the front and rear.

Apart from the characteristics enumerated above, it also bears noting that all the chairs excavated from the Pan Hui tomb had seats made from a single board, which may constitute a simplified design. The seats of the chairs excavated from the Pan Yunzheng tomb, however, were of woven rattan above and palms below, with supporting boards underneath. This is widely seen in the furniture that has been preserved over the generations, which indicates that the chair seats of the Ming period were not uniformly the soft seats made of rattan and palm.

Tables

Ming tables could be divided into two types—the *zhuo* and the *an*. A table with recessed legs was called *an* to distinguish it from the *zhuo,* which has legs at the corners and a waist. The construction and function of the *an* were established as early as the Han period (206 B.C.–220 A.D.). For instance, the *Later Han Record: Life of Lian Hong* mentioned that "the wife bringing the food dares not face her husband directly, but raises the *an* to the height of her eyebrows." This refers to a small *an* used for food, which was a tray with legs. Again, in the *Dong Guan Hushu* (Dong Guan Han Records), it is recorded that "Lady Han was about to partake of a drink, when the retainer came in to report on business, and she rose in anger and smashed the *an*." Here, the *an* refers to the desk, which was much larger.

But what about the kinds of *an* of the Ming period? The archaeological finds supply important clues. The most important feature of the *an* excavated at the Pan Yunzheng tomb (cat. 30d) is their size. They were quite large and their surfaces were very wide. Evidently they were used for calligraphy or painting rather than eating. Such desks have also been found among the furniture that has been preserved.

Three other model *an* were unearthed from tombs in the Shanghai area, but these were small and narrow. They were matched with benches when excavated, which indicates that they were used for eating. We can see examples of this in such Ming paintings as Zhou Chen's *Chunshan You Qi Tu* (Scenes of a Spring Outing on Horseback), in which guests are depicted holding wine cups, seated on benches, facing each other across such an *an.*

Chests

Few genuine Ming chests have been preserved and handed down. With the added consideration of the fact that little changed in the design of chests from the Ming to the Qing period (1644–1911), it becomes difficult to date those that are extant. Excavated Ming chests as a whole tend to be rectangular in shape. The six miniature Ming chests in the Shanghai Museum's collection were excavated from three different tombs. Of them, those excavated from the late-Ming tombs of Pan Yunzheng and Pan Hui (cat. 30h) are rectangular, as are the accessories, such as the clapper and the front clasp of the hardware. The early Ming pottery chest, although rectangular in form, has clasps in long strips. Thus we may deduce that the hardware on Ming-period chests evolved from long strips to rectangles. The rectangular clappers were often seen in illustrations to Ming stories, while the cloud- shaped *ruyi* clappers were unknown. It is this writer's opinion that the latter *ruyi* clappers were in vogue during the Qing period. But further excavations are required to verify whether this transition occurred during the Ming or the early Qing.

Furniture Arrangement

Although Ming furniture had not yet evolved to the point of being produced in complete sets, as they would be in the Qing period, theories of how furniture affects interior environment and atmosphere were already being put forth during the Ming period. For instance, Wen Zhenheng, in his *Zhang Wu Zhi* (A Treatise on Superfluous Things), wrote: "The methods of arranging furniture are varied. Some are simple, others complicated. They also differ from winter to summer. The high-roofed hall, the spacious pavilion, rooms of various sizes—each has its own advantages for placing furniture." In the Ming period, articles of furniture were positioned according to their functions.

More than ten types of furniture were excavated from Pan Yunzheng's tomb, all of which fall into two categories in terms of function: those accommodating sleeping, such as the alcove bed, matched with garment rack, washbasin holder, chamber pot, chest, cabinet, etc, in sum, those comprising a bedroom set, the remaining pieces served the activities that took place in the study—the daybed and the large desk for painting and calligraphy. *Zhang Wu Zhi* describes the interior of a Ming hall: a long *an,* with lamps hanging on either side, sometimes a square table, with chairs on either side, in front of the *an*. No *an,* square tables, or matching chairs were unearthed in the excavations of the Pan tomb, thus we may deduce that the excavated furniture from that tomb was mainly for bedroom and study. By consulting historical records and illustrations to Ming stories, we could reproduce the living environment of Pan Yunzheng as it had been during his lifetime.

To judge from illustrations, the alcove bed was always positioned in the secluded portion of a room, against the wall. The alcove bed from Wang Xijue's tomb supports this hypothesis as well. When discovered, it was placed in the outer coffin along with other pieces of furniture, all in their original positions. The bed, facing the door, was at the top axis of the room, with a table for offerings at its head and a garment rack to the right. This arrangement of furniture, with the bed as the axis, situates the other furniture in such a manner as to radiate out from the bed.

During the Ming period, no rigid rules guided the use of chairs. In general, the Song-period practice of placing one table with one chair, or one table with two chairs was maintained. One may see such arrangements for both studies and bedrooms in illustrations to Ming stories. Household items such as a lamp would also have been placed on the table.

The garment rack was an indispensable part of bedroom or study furniture during the Ming period. The example excavated from Wang Xijue's tomb was placed on one side of the alcove bed, in keeping with illustrations to Ming stories (see cat. 29 and 30k).

Standing cabinets were called *chu* in the south. These large, tall pieces opened at the front, while the unadorned board at the rear usually was placed against the wall. The cabinets could also hold odds and ends, and they were often depicted in shops in book illustrations. The cabinets in the bedroom held clothing and are usually referred to as "clothes cabinets." The example excavated at the Pan tomb was placed to one side of the alcove bed, against the wall. To this day, the peasants in the Shanghai suburbs still arrange their furniture according to this pattern.

The chest is also used to store clothing, and Ming illustrations suggest that it was invariably set against the wall. Symmetry in furniture arrangement was in vogue during the Ming, and the chest on one side of the alcove bed balanced the clothes cabinet on the other side appropriately.

As components of the bedroom furnishings, the washbasin stand and towel rack were indispensable for personal toilette. In Ming illustrations, a brass basin was placed on the stand while a brass mirror and a wooden comb lay by the side. The brass basin held water and the towel was hung on its rack after using. The basin, stand, and towel rack were always placed together to one side of the bed.

The charcoal burner, which was used for heating, is a household item often seen in Ming illustrations. During the Ming period, charcoal burners were sometimes placed directly underfoot and sometimes in the center of the room. A kettle often would be placed on top, thus combining the functions of heating the room and making boiled water.

The foot-washing basin and chamber pot were also essential household items of ancient times, and were the items most frequently discovered among excavated furniture. They were also found in the tomb of Zhu Tan, who died in Shandong in early Ming times. Because of their obvious inelegance, they were invariably placed beneath the bed or tucked away in corners.

Fig. 2. Model study furniture from the tomb of Pan Yunzheng. Shanghai Museum, Shanghai.

In general, we could say that Ming furniture had yet to be formed into a uniform system and style. The common people could not afford furniture in matching sets, and one item often served many functions. Only the halls and residences of aristocrats could boast complete sets of furniture. But how were these items placed? Presently more than ten types of objects have been retrieved from the Pan Yunzheng tomb. Using the guidelines set forth above, the writer has arrived at the arrangements illustrated in an attempt to restore the bedroom (fig. 1) and study (fig. 2) of Pan Yunzheng.

From *Xi Xiang Ji* (Tale of the Western Chamber),
Xiang Xue Ju edition, 1614.

One Ming Gentleman's Notions on Room Order: Selections from *Zhang Wu Zhi*—A Treatise on Superfluous Things, by Wen Zhenheng (1585–1645)[1]

Translation by Huajing Xiu Maske

Positioning and Arranging

The methods of arranging furniture are varied. Some are simple, others complicated. They also differ from winter to summer. The high-roofed hall, the spacious pavilion, rooms of various sizes—each has its own advantages for placing furniture. Likewise, books and ceremonial wares should also be suitably arranged so that they create a scene resembling lofty clouds, firmiana trees, and ancient rocks. With only a small table and a couch-bed installed, visitors can recognize a room's charm. Thus people with refined taste can make the entrance of their house appear cultured and tasteful. If, however, chickens and livestock are raised in the front courtyard, with flowers and rocks planted pretentiously in the back courtyard, then the situation is worse than dust covering the table. The surrounding walls have a desolate air. This is the tenth position.[2]

The Sitting Table

A table made of a solid plank of wood (*tianran ji*) should be placed to the left of the room and facing the east. It is not to be near the window, but should be protected from the wind and sun.[3] Upon it there should rest an old inkstone (*jiu yan*), a brush pot (*bitong*), a brush (*bi*), a water holder (*shuizhongcheng*), and a mountain inkstone (*yanshan*). Ancient people placed the inkstone on the left part of the table. The ink should also be put under the lantern in such a way that its reflection does not bother the eyes. On the table there should be paperweights (*zhen zhi*) both for books and painting albums. These should be frequently dusted and polished so that they look as bright and clear as a mirror.

Seats

Couch-beds made of Xiang bamboo (*xiangzhu ta*)[4] and Zen chairs (*chan yi*)[5] may be used as seats. In the winter, cushions made of antique brocade or tiger skin may be applied on these seats.

Chairs (*yi*) , Couch-beds (*ta*), Screen (*ping*), and Supporting Stands (*jia*)

Only four chairs and a couch-bed should occupy a study. Others, such as the ancient *xuni* seat (*gu xunizuo*), low couch-bed (*duan ta*), short table (*ai ji*), or wall table (*bi ji*), might suit a room as well. Avoid arranging several chairs in a row along the wall. Only one panel of a screen should be installed. Shelves and cabinets should be installed to keep books and paintings in order. However, there should not be too many of them; otherwise, the room looks like a bookstore.

Hanging Paintings

It is better to hang paintings up high. Only one painting should be hung in a room.

It is regarded as vulgar to hang paintings on two walls or hang two paintings symmetrically at both left and right. Long scrolls should be hung on high walls. It is not advisable to use a bamboo hanging stick (*ai hua zhu qu*) to hang paintings. There should be exotic rocks or a potted landscape of seasonal flowers on the painting table. Red-lacquer stands should be strictly avoided. Large horizontal scrolls (*da hengpi*) should be hung in halls, while small landscape paintings and bird-and-flower (*xiaojing huaniao*) subjects should be hung in rooms. Single strips (*dan tiao*) and fan paintings (*shanmian*), as well as square pictures (*dou fang*), are rather unseemly. The saying that paintings should not be placed in front of real landscape can also be wrong.

Incense Burners

Upon the usual sitting table should stand a low, square altar on which will be an incense burner (*lu*), a big incense-powder box (*xiang he*), two small pieces of powder, and unpowdered incense sticks, chips of aloes wood or gharu wood (*chen xiang bing*), and an incense tool box (*jin ping*). Never use two burners in one room. Burners should not be put on the painting table or placed symmetrically with vases and boxes. A ceramic burner is suitable for the summer while brass [bronze] is appropriate for the winter.

Vases

Vases of various shapes should be placed on low stands of suitable sizes. In spring and summer it is better to use brass vases, while in autumn and winter ceramic ones are best. Big vases look harmonious in large halls and small vases appear more attractive in rooms. Bronze and ceramic vases should be treasured above gold and silver ones. Avoid using vases with rings or in pairs. Flowers in the vase should be delicate and slim instead of petty and varied. If just one blossom is to be put in the vase, then a rare and exotic type should be chosen. If two are to be inserted, then they should be arranged in a harmonious way such that they do not appear too rigid, nor should they all be of equal height. Only one or two types [of flowers and plants] may be used. If more are added, they become as disorderly as a wine shop. However, autumnal flowers in small vases are the exception. Flowers should be put in places with windows open, because otherwise they become withered as soon as incense smoke touches them. The narcissus is particularly sensitive [to incense smoke].

Small Rooms

It is advised not to put too many tables and couch-beds in small rooms. However, an antique writing table with narrow edges should suit the center of a room very well. Small and tasteful things such as brushes, inkstones, incense-powder boxes, or incense burners should be displayed upon it. A small stone table should be placed separately for a tea set. One small couch-bed is needed for reclining or for sitting cross-legged. There is no need to hang paintings. Old and fantastic rocks also serve a good purpose, as does a small cabinet in which a small gilded Buddha sits.

The Bedroom

Wooden floors in the bedroom can be vulgar, but will do as long as the room is located in a dry area. There must not be any colored pictures or painted surfaces inside. Facing the south should stand a sleeping couch-bed (*shui ta*), behind which some space is left for displaying an incense burner, a garment rack (*yi jia*), a chamber pot, a washbasin (*shu yi*), a cosmetics box (*xiang he*), and a reading lantern (*shu deng*). A bare, small table should be put in front of the couch-bed. There should be two small, square stools (*fang wu*) and a small cabinet for keeping incense and articles of amusement. The room should be clean and elegantly simple. Even the slightest touch of stylish adornment would make it look like the women's quarters, which is definitely not appropriate for a hermit who supposedly sleeps with clouds and dreams of the moon. There should, of course, be a bed along the wall, so it is possible for friends to stay and exchange conversation at night. Below the bed there should be a drawer for shoes and socks. Not many flowers and plants are needed. If any, a rare and mysterious type seems most appropriate, and it should be accompanied by a stone from Ying.[6]

Pavilion (*ting xie*)

Since pavilions do not provide shelter from wind and rain, it is not advisable to place good-quality furniture and utensils there. However, vulgar ones are unbearable. Therefore, an old lacquered table with square surface and thick foot is most appropriate. It should be simple and natural as well. Smooth and short lake rocks should be scattered around for seats. Stone stools and tile stools should not be placed here. Furthermore, a red framework should not be placed on top of the bricks.

The Grand Room (*chang shi*)

The long summer perfectly suits the grand room. Lattices are all taken off the windows. The room is completely shaded with Chinese firmiana trees in front and bamboo in the rear. The room should have a big and long wooden table in the center, accompanied by long couch-beds on either side. No screen is necessary, because good paintings tend to get very dry in the summer, plus, since the back of the room is thoroughly open to the outside, there is no proper place to hang them. Against the north window should be placed a Xiang bamboo couch-bed, bedded with a bamboo mat, for reclining. On the table, a big inkstone and a blue-green water basin should be displayed. Such things as ceremonial wares need to be of large size as well. By the table, one or two pots of orchids should be exhibited. There is no harm in placing extra miniature landscapes formed with rare peaks, old trees, clear brooks, and white pebbles. Bamboo curtains hanging down around the room, will make it appear cool and refreshing.

Notes:

1. Wen Zhenheng wrote *Zhang Wu Zhi* c. 1615–20.

2. Translator's note: meaning obscure.

3. *Tianran ji* would seem to imply that this is a desk, though desks would usually have been placed near a window for better light.

4. Translator's note: Xiang bamboo is also called Xiaoxiang bamboo. It is a type of mottled bamboo that grows in south China.

5. Translator's note: a type of chair used by Buddhist monks to sit for meditation.

6. Translator's note: stone from Ying (*Ying shi*) was produced in an area between Hanguang county and Chen Yang county in Guangdong province. It is a variously colored rock, with peaks and hollows, and is taken from a river.

Catalogue of the exhibition

by Nancy Berliner

Notes regarding the catalogue entries

Few dated pieces of Chinese furniture are extant, and because many generations adhered to classical styles, exact dating is not yet possible. Unless otherwise noted, each of the following pieces dates from the sixteenth to the seventeenth centuries.

I have avoided such European- and American-devised names as *horseshoe chair* and *yokeback chair,* which, though descriptive, stray too far from the Chinese terms for these chair types. When Chinese words in italics follow English terms, they are transliterations of the common Chinese terms for these types of furniture. It is often the case that a variety of Chinese terms have been used, in different times and in different regions, to designate one type of furniture. I have included all of these terms.

The line following the dimensions denotes the type of wood from which the piece is constructed. During the late-Ming period, hardwoods became extremely popular for furniture. The most preferred woods at this time were *huali* (flowering pear), burl, and the very dark and very dense *zitan* (purple sandalwood). A blonder *huali,* of which many late-Ming and early Qing furnishings were constructed, was more recently given the appellation *huanghuali* (yellow flowering pear).

All objects are from private collections unless otherwise indicated.

1. Screen [*pingfeng*] 黃花梨 屏風

55⅜ in. (h) × 33½ in. (w) × 18 in. (d)
Huanghuali

*I block out the midday brightness with a
screen depicting dark woods,
Burn a stick of heavy incense, nursing my
hangover.*[1]

*The house in which the Fang family lived only
had three buildings. In the back area was the
kitchen and stove and the bedrooms. The
center area was for greeting guests. In the
small rooms on either side were piles of rice
and grasses for brushwood. The first area
abutted the main street. Right in the center
were two large doors. Within the doors, block-
ing the hall was a screen. The chambers
beside it were extraneous rooms in which
were piled miscellaneous things.*[2]

*Tao Ji went up to the small building and
carefully inspected the doors, the windows,
the lattice, the bed, the screens, the chairs
and the table. He became utterly excited. He
turned to the couple. "This bedroom building
is definitely the place where I spent my childhood. I see it often in my dreams when I
sleep."*[3]

Screens were as fundamental as any other
piece of furniture in a Chinese household.
Pingfeng, the Chinese word for screen, literally means to shield from the wind, and
from the Zhou period on, screens were a
form of portable architecture. Even in the
Ming, screens were not merely background
decorations, but essential props for
deflecting the wind, creating privacy, maintaining geomantic harmony as prescribed
by the Chinese science of *fengshui,* and
expressing status. They were used in all
areas of a domestic household. In Ming fiction, servants or women are often
described as peeking out from behind
screens to watch clandestine activities or
to eavesdrop on conversations restricted
to the menfolk.

Screens were made in a variety of
sizes, from several inches to several feet in
height. Small screens for tables shielded
inked inkstones from drafts and kept the
liquid from drying. Larger screens were
placed at room entrances as well as
behind the seat of the most highly hon-
ored person present.

The large, flat surface of a screen bears
obvious potential space for decoration.

Since the earliest screens, this surface has
been used for paintings and calligraphy. A
Northern Wei period red-lacquer screen
found in the tomb of Sima Jinlong in
Datong, Shanxi province, depicts scenes
from morality tales.[4] A Song painting at the
Museum of Fine Arts, Boston, shows a
screen protecting a young woman seated
at an outdoor table, the frames of which
are filled completely with ink-delineated
waves. The framed panel of the screen
included in this exhibition may have held a
slab of marble, a painting on silk or paper,
or even a carved-clay plaque.

In addition to decorations within the
framed panel, the frames of screens were
often also elaborately carved. The pierced
carving around the sides of this screen
depicts mythological and auspicious creatures.

Construction

This screen consists of two parts—the
inserted flat screen itself and its base. The
flat screen easily slips out for convenient
moving.

The frame members of the panel are
mitered with through tenons that are
exposed on the top and bottom but not
the sides. Horizontal and vertical rails
divide the space within the frame, creating
five openings: two horizontal and two vertical openings surrounding the fifth, central
opening, which is square. The vertical rails
meet the horizontal rails with through
tenons. The horizontal rails also meet the
frame members with through tenons.

The inside of the center opening is a
rabbet, made to accept an inset, which is
no longer in place. Two sliding tenons on
the upper part of the vertical rails would
have supported the decorative panel. Two
mortises on the lower horizontal rail
accepted the bottom of that panel. All the
rails have full double beads down their
centers. Floating panels with pierced, raised
carving fill the vertical and horizontal
openings between the rails.

The frame panel drops into a groove
inside the two upright stiles of the base
stand. On the base, the upright stiles
through tenon into the feet and are supported on either side by pierced, carved
spandrels that tenon into the stile.

Pipa Ji (Story of the Lute), Wanli (1573–1620)
Ji Yi Tang edition.

Three horizontal rails form two horizontal openings across the width of the
stand. The openings are filled with floating
panels with raised, pierced carving. Below
the lowest rail an outward-angled apron
stretches the width of the stand and is
notched into channels in the stile and the
feet. The two feet on either side are solid
blocks with raised carving. The front apron
has raised carving and bead, but the rear
apron is plain, with no carving and only a
beaded edge.

1. Pi Rixiu (c. 833(?)–883), "Impromptu on a Hangover."
Trans. from Jonathan Chaves, *The Columbia Book of Later
Chinese Poetry.* New York: Columbia University Press, 1986,
p. 290.

2. Tianran Chisou (Foolish Old Man of Nature; pseud. of
Langxian, c.1627), *Shi Dian Tou* (Rocks Nod Their Heads),
late Ming. Reprint. Jilin: Wenshi Chubanshe, 1986, p. 74.

3. Li Yu (1611–80), "Sheng Wo Lou" (The House of My
Birth), in *Shi Er Lou* (Twelve Buildings). Taibei: Chang Ge
Chubanshe, 1975, p. 326.

4. "Shanxi Datongshi Bowuguan, Shanxi Datong Shijiazhai
Bei Wei Sima Jinlong Mu" (The Northern Wei Tomb of
Sima Jinlong in Shijia Village, Datong County, Shanxi
Province). *Wenwu* 1972, no. 3, pp. 20–29.

2. Folding Stool [*ma zha*] 黃花梨 馬閘

39 in. (h) × 15 in. (w) × 15 in. (d)
Huanghuali with iron mounts

A barbarian bed is made to swivel shut with intersecting legs, and has ropes threaded across for a seat. It is able to shrink in size instantly, and the seat only weighs a few catties. It is said that Minghuang [Emperor Tang Xuanzong, 685–762] traveled frequently. When his officials or attendants were stopping in the wilderness or when the emperor was climbing a mountain, they could not always stand, but there was nothing to allow them to rest their bodies. Thus, this [folding chair] was invented and at that time it was called the "wandering in the distance" seat.[1]

While the folding-stool form has been a basic utensil in Chinese households and on the road for almost two millennia, and in the countryside continues to be so even today, by the late Ming it probably was not a seat that was offered to important visitors or hosts. In the Northern Song painting *Bei Qi Jiaoshu Tu* (Collating the Texts; Museum of Fine Arts, Boston), said to be a copy of a Tang work, one of the distinguished scholars depicted is shown seated on a folding stool, writing on a paper held by a servant. But, by the late Ming, paintings and woodblock prints rarely depict figures seated on these eight-rod conveniences. Nor are there many clay or wooden models of folding stools in the excavated sets of Ming tomb furnishings that attempt to simulate luxurious households for the deceased.[2] In the *San Cai Tu Hui* (Pictorial Encyclopedia of Heaven, Earth, and Man, compiled by Wang Siyin and published in 1610), the section defining furniture types does not include the folding stool, though it does depict folding chairs with backs and four-legged stools. Artists and writers were more anxious to portray the other intricate and complex furniture types that had evolved by the seventeenth century rather than this ancient forebear.

Despite the lack of imagery, enough folding stools are still extant to testify to their wide employment in the Ming period. Most likely they were used for temporary seating when traveling. Alighting from a sedan chair to rest on his way to a far off town, an official may have sat upon his folding stool, which had been carried by a servant, and gaze at the mountain scenery.

Indeed, a woodblock-print illustration from the Wanli period (1573–1620) *Lie Nu Zhuan* (Biographies of Exemplary Women) illustrates such a circumstance.

The amount of hardware on this piece demonstrates that it was made to withstand rough use and travel. Metal mounts protected the footrest from being worn down, more hardware reinforced the joinery holding the legs to the seat frame and to the base, and still further mounts ensured that the hinge would open and close easily.

Construction

The seat is constructed of two parallel members between which woven rattan or palm fibers were originally stretched, then threaded through a line of holes (drilled in two directions) along the inner edges of the top parallel members. The facade of the front member is carved in relief with two facing dragons and a scrolling vine. A molded top edge and beaded bottom and side edges surround the front surface. The rear seat member is distinguished only by a scrolling vine carved in relief and beaded edges similar to those on the sides.

The four round leg members through tenon into the ends of the seat members at forty-five-degree angles. They cross each other at their centers and through tenon into the base members at opposite ends. Where the two legs at either side cross each other, the round surfaces become flattened to allow for smoother working movement in folding the stool. The crossed legs are attached by a metal pin with heads on either side of the leg. Elaborate cloud-headed metal mounts on the legs keep the pin from wearing down the wood. Similarly styled hardware wraps down the legs and around the base members.

The footrest tenons into the legs at either side. The front of the footrest sits on an apron with two legs, which are separate and attach to the apron by a mitered bridle joint, the legs through tenoning to the top of the footrest. Elaborately designed metal hardware covers the footrest to prevent it from being worn down.

Lie Nu Zhuan (Biographies of Exemplary Women), Wanli edition.

1. From Tao Gu (903–970), *Qing Yi Lu*, as quoted in Zhu Jiajin, "Random Talks on Chairs and Stools and Methods of Arrangements." *Wenwu Can Kao Ziliao* no. 6 (1959).

2. Except for one carried over the shoulder of an attendant, the Museum of Classical Chinese Furniture's plentiful collection of miniature pottery tomb furniture does not include any folding stools.

3. Folding Round-back Chair
[*jiaoyi*] 黃花梨 交椅

39 in. (h) × 15 in. (w) × 15 in. (d)
Huanghuali with brass mounts
Collection of Nelson-Atkins Museum of Art, Kansas City

In the reception room, ablaze with lamps and candles, the table was laid with a full complement of wine and delicacies, a single folding chair at its head. Not until Ximen Qing assumed the place of honor was a jug of wine broached and decanted.[1]

Developed during the Song period, the folding chair with rounded crestrail had become by the Ming a designated seat of honor in the official household. Woodblock prints and paintings often depict important dignitaries seated on such chairs presiding over official assemblies in reception halls. These chairs were not sturdy or comfortable enough for casual gatherings of friends or for relaxing in bedrooms. Nor, apparently, were they appropriate for Buddhist monks or priests who usually sat with their legs folded, a position that would have been difficult to assume and perhaps unstable to maintain in a folding chair. This was the chair of the emperor or those to whom he had delegated power. Even through the Qing, when use of these chairs waned, the Qianlong emperor (1736–96) sat for a portrait in a highly ornamented example,[2] and ancestral portraits often depicted the deceased—who, as spirits, occupied an honorable and powerful position—sitting in folding chairs with rounded crestrails. A Ming portrait of four generations of a family shows nine people, men and women, all seated in folding chairs with rounded crestrails that are draped with brocade covers.[3]

This chair is distinguished by the fine relief carving of scrolling vines and flowers on the back splat. Several peaks of a mountain range are depicted at the lower end of the splat. Relief carving of similar scrolling vines and flowers also decorates the front surface of the front seat frame member. An elongated and animated dragon, carved in relief, twists along each terminating end of the crestrail, his face turned inward toward the sitter. This last detail is reminiscent of Ming woodblock prints where dragons may be seen carved on the rails and arms of chairs intended for illustrious personages. An imperial, Qianlong-period, lacquer, round-back folding chair (Palace Museum, Beijing) has such gold dragon heads at the ends of its armrests.

The metalwork on this chair is particularly unusual. Instead of the brass typically used on furniture, the hardware is made of iron inlaid with silver designs of scrolling vines and flowers, echoing the relief carving on the back splat. Such ironwork only appears on several other folding armchairs, one in the Museum of Classical Chinese Furniture, one in the collection of Mrs. Chen Mengjia in Beijing, and one in the Royal Ontario Museum in Toronto. Sarah Handler has suggested that the first two of these, along with this chair, possibly were produced in the same workshop.[4]

Construction

The continuous round crestrail is composed of three curved sections joined together by half-lapped scarf joints, each with a single peg. Metal bands around the crestrail reinforce the joints and prevent them from loosening during travel and rough usage. The crestrail ends protrude over the arm supports, with an exaggerated outward curve.

The C-curved splat, with flanges decorating its upper portion and a relief carved design over its entire front, is constructed of a single piece of wood.

A serpentine-shaped brace, tenoned into the bottom surface of the crestrail and further supported by a spandrel, stretches back, around, and down to meet the back seat frame and tenon into the outer leg. A second, larger spandrel supports this deep C-curve, and a silver-ornamented iron mount further secures it. The curved crestrail is further supported by two straight metal rods, one on either side, that tenon into the crestrail above and into the serpentine brace below.

The back seat frame tenons into the outer legs on either end. The front seat frame, which has relief carving and a cusped outline, is supported by the inner legs, which tenon into its bottom surface at an angle.

Like the folding stool (cat. 2), the two legs cross each other at their centers and through tenon into the base members at opposite ends. Where the two legs cross each other at either side, the round surfaces become flattened to allow for smoother working movement in folding the chair. The crossed legs are attached together by a metal pin. Silver-ornamented

Xiu Xin Bian Chuxiang Nan Ke Meng Ji, Wanli edition.

iron mounts on the legs keep the pin from wearing down the wood. Similarly styled hardware is used to strengthen the legs' joints to the base members.

The footrest tenons into the legs at either side. The front of the footrest sits on an apron with two legs. Elaborate metal hardware covers the footrest to prevent it from being worn down.

1. *Jin Ping Mei*, from David Tod Roy, trans., *The Plum in the Golden Vase*, vol. 1. Princeton, New Jersey: Princeton University Press, 1993, chapter 16, p. 333.

2. In *Qingdai Gongting Hui Hua* (Qing Palace Painting). Beijing: Wenwu Pub. Co., 1993.

3. *Four Generations of Zhou Yong's Family*, by an anonymous Ming painter. In Liang Baiquan, *Selected Chinese Portrait Paintings from the Nanjing Museum*. Hong Kong: Tai Yip/Cultural Relics Pub. Co., 1987.

4. Sarah Handler, "The Elegant Vagabond: The Chinese Folding Armchair." *Orientations*, vol. 23, no. 1 (1/92), pp. 90–96.

4. Garden Stool [*shi dun*] 石墩

19 in. (h) × 12 in. (w) × 12 in. (d)
Marble

Wu Song said: "It's just that they say I have no strength. But since they've said that, yesterday I saw that stone stool [shi dun] in front of the Hall of the Heavenly King. About how many pounds do you think it weighs?" She En said: "I'm afraid it must weigh four or five hundred pounds!" Wu Song said: "Let's go see. Wu Song doesn't know if he could move it or not."[1]

Early Chinese paintings, such as *Scholars in a Garden,* a Five Dynasties work by Zhou Wenju (c. 970), often depict human figures seated on natural rocks. With the increased emphasis on furniture and its construction during the Song, stones were soon being carved and shaped to imitate more refined seating arrangements.

Stone furniture was commonly placed in gardens and courtyards, which are integral to traditional Chinese architecture, thus reducing the amount of indoor furniture that had to be moved for an outdoor gathering. Paintings and woodblock prints from the Ming period frequently include finely carved stone drum stools as well as stone tables and benches. Stone benches in the front courtyard of the Lu family residence in Shaoxing, built in the Jiajing reign period (1522–66), and a stone incense table at the Bao Guo Si temple in Ningbo, testify to the existence of such outdoor furnishings.

The benches in Shaoxing and the incense table in Ningbo both imitate wooden carpentry techniques. This stone stool instead mimics a stool construction of rush. Due to the lack of long-term durability of the latter material, no Ming examples of rush stools are extant. However, numerous late-Ming woodblock prints and texts, as well as paintings from as early as the Song, demonstrate that these lightweight rush stools were another common form of casual outdoor seating. As was done with many wooden chairs, fine fabrics were occasionally thrown over these seats to make them more comfortable. The Song painting *Shiba Xueshi Tu* (Eighteen Scholars), at the National Palace Museum, Taiwan, depicts one such dressed rush chair, but in a Wanli illustrated version of *Shui Hu Zhuan* (The Water Margin), the famous libidinous couple Ximen Qing and Pan Jinlian sit outdoors on plain, bare rush stools, entranced with one another at their first encounter.

In *Zhang Wu Zhi* (Treatise on Superfluous Things), the Ming writer Wen Zhenheng (1585–1645) describes how to make a *zuodun* (sitting stool): "In the winter, use rushes to make a stool one *chi* two *cun* high. On all sides, the silk bindings should be fine and dense. To make it especially strong and solid, use the wooden seat board from a carriage to support the top."[2]

Construction

The rush material generated a form and construction completely distinct from wooden carpentry. Instead of straight wooden legs, a series of circular rush rings create a support for the seat. Instead of complex joinery, fibers—of silk or rush itself—are used to fasten together the parts of the stool. Bundles of rush are tied into eight vertical, interlocking rings that are subsequently bound one to the other at their outermost points with a smaller horizontal ring. These vertical rings form a circle that is then fastened to additional horizontal rings at the top and bottom. A flat, circular piece of wood atop the whole structure forms a seat, and another below becomes the base.

The stool was carved entirely from one piece of stone in imitation of this rush structure.

1. *Shui Hu Zhuan* (The Water Margin), in the *Shuihu Quan Zhuan* edition. Beijing: Rong Yu Tang, 1954, p. 443.

2. Wen Zhenheng, *Zhang Wu Zhi* (Treatise on Superfluous Things, 1615–20). Reprinted in *Ouya Tang Cong Shu.* Taibei: Hualian Chubanshe, 1965, vol. 261.

Shui Hu Zhuan (The Water Margin), Wanli Rong Yu Tang edition.

5. Pair of Drum Stools [*gudun, xiudun*] 黃花梨 鼓墩，繡墩

19 in. (h) × 11 in. (w) × 11 in. (d)
Huanghuali

From the right and the left, they were welcomed into the hall. The king went up onto the throne. Below him on his left was placed an embroidered xiudun *[drum stool]. He invited the* jieyuan *[top candidate in the provincial level civil exam] to have a seat. Yuan bowed down again and said, "With the king before me, how do I dare sit?"*[1]

In a situation where a lower-ranking individual paid a call on a higher-ranking host, the more exalted person usually would be seated in a grand armchair or a rounded-crestrail chair, while the visitor would be offered a stool. The disadvantages of the stool were multifold: it had no back splat to lean against, no arm supports, and no footrest. But sitting on seats without back supports was not considered a discomfort and much leisure time among the elite seems also to have been spent seated on elegant drum stools. Late-Ming woodblock prints depict friends playing chess, women sewing, and companions drinking and dining while seated on such stools.

Drum stools made out of a variety of materials were a popular form of both indoor and outdoor casual seating. Artisans of all types produced these stools from materials as diverse as celadon, porcelain, stone, wood, and even cloisonné. They were variously called *zuodun* (sitting stool), *gudun* (drum stool), and *xiudun* (embroidered stool), so named because they were often covered with embroidered textiles for extra comfort. Likenesses of these rectangular fabrics are often carved as decoration on stone drum stools, which even detail semblances of the brass rings attached at each corner of the fabric in order to weight it down.

This stool derives its design elements from two divergent traditions: drums, and rush or bamboo stools. Characteristic of many drum stools is the row of decorative circular bumps on the seat frame members just below the top edge. These bumps are descendants of the nailheads that hold down the leather on an actual drum. While they have no practical function on the wooden stool, carpenters felt compelled to carve these decorative nails. The band of nails was often also carved into the stone, drum-shaped column sup-

ports in architecture. The central circular struts, and the smaller round rings between them, originate from the rush or silk rings on rush and bamboo stools.

Construction

The seat is constructed of four rounded frame members—held together by double finger joints—encircling a central circular floating panel. For extra support, a center transverse brace crosses under the circular panel and is attached to it by a sliding dovetail and double tenons into the seat frame members. The brace goes across the wood grain to keep the seat panel flat. The legs meet the seat at the double finger joints with a front-mitered lap joint and a rear mortise-and-tenon on either side, reinforcing the joints holding together the seat frame members.

In the openings between the legs are a series of rounded interlocking strapworks that intersect at a small, rectangular O-shape. The strapwork on two opposing sides was replaced.

The circular base is constructed of four rounded members joined together by a half-lapped scarf joint with a single wedge tenon. Below the base are four feet attached by a front lap joint with a single tenon mortised into the base at points off the joints of the base.

All parts have beaded edges.

1. Feng Menglong, "Li Gongzi Jiu She Huo Chengxin" (Prince Li Saves a Snake and Achieves Satisfaction). In *Gu Jin Xiao Shuo* (Stories Old and New). Beijing: Remin Chubanshe,1984, p. 541.

Xi Xiang Ji (Tale of the Western Chamber), 1614 Xiang Xue Ju edition.

6. Pair of Stools [*dun*] 樹根 墩

18¼ in. (h) × 16½ in. (w) × 16½ in. (d)
Rootwood

These stools combine a reminiscence of the drum-stool shape with Buddhist and Taoist associations of the natural root material.

As early as the Five Dynasties period, these furnishings seemingly created by nature carried enough prestige and symbolic meaning that the palace artist Zhou Wenju (c. 970) painted the emperor, Minghuang, seated on a large root chair, accompanied by Buddhist priests and monks, playing chess on a board placed on a root table.[1] Many of the people portrayed sitting on large, fanciful root furniture were, in fact, Taoist or Buddhist devotees. A Buddhist figure is pictured sitting on a root chair in the 1173–76 scroll from Dali, Yunnan.[2] In scrolls illustrating the theft of the renowned Wang Xizhi calligraphy of the Orchid Pavilion Preface, its owner, the monk Bian Cai, is often depicted sitting on a large, root, official's hat chair constructed of naturally formed, unrefined wood. He is depicted thus in "Xiaoyi Obtaining the Lanting Manuscript by Trickery" (Freer Gallery, Washington, D.C.), a sixteenth-century work by an anonymous artist that shows this event.[3]·

The connection between tree roots and Buddhism probably derives from Buddhist and Taoist notions of flowing with, rather than against, the tides of nature. The root material also conveys the humble attitudes of these religious adherents. In Ming woodblock prints, peasants and poorer members of society are often portrayed sitting on simpler root stools. By the late Ming such humbleness and closeness to natural order was a desirable aesthetic. In a portrait by Jia Ruilin, the great Ming connoisseur and collector Xiang Yuanbian (1525–90) sits in a root chair next to a root table.[4]

Construction

As with rushes and other nontimber materials, creating furniture from roots necessitates its own peculiar construction techniques. In his pursuit of naturalism, the carpenter attempted to create the illusion that each stool consisted of one perfectly shaped root. In fact, however, each stool is made of several pieces of root ingeniously fitted together.

The stools are both fabricated of several pieces of root, joined by wooden pegs (and, in some places, later reinforced with metal nails) to form the shape of a drum with a hollow interior. The tops are constructed of one piece of root that laps over the side edges, where further pieces of root are joined to it. All joins are completely disguised by a coat of lacquer.

1. *Minghuang Playing Chess*, now in the National Palace Museum, Beijing. Published in *Gugong Minghua Sanbaizhong* (Three Hundred Masterpieces of Chinese Painting in the Palace Museum). Taizhong: National Palace Museum and National Central Museum, 1959.

2. Published in Helen B. Chapin, "A Long Roll of Buddhist Images," *Artibus Asiae*, vol. XXXII, 4 (1970), pp. 259–306.

3. Thomas Lawton, *Chinese Figure Painting*. Washington, D.C.: Smithsonian Institution, 1973, p. 77.

4. Reproduced in Michel Beurdeley, *Chinese Furniture*. Tokyo and New York: Kodansha International, 1979.

7. Pair of Side Chairs with Protruding Crestrails [*kaobeiyi, dengguayi*] 黃花梨 靠背椅，燈挂椅

47 in. (h) × 23 in. (w) × 17 in. (d)

Huanghuali

Wei Gao took the fan, looked at it, and immediately began jumping about, shouting: "It's beautiful, beautiful. Brilliant." Yu Xiao said: "Why are you wildly shouting like that?" Wei Gao did not answer. He just closed the study door, dragged over a chair, took Yu Xiao's hand and said, "Please sit, so that I can better share a cup with you."[1]

The Chinese word for this type of chair distinctly describes what differentiates it from stools: *kaobeiyi* translates to mean a chair against which the back can lean. This chair allowed the sitter to lean and also to sit straighter than on a stool. This advantage in comfort no doubt attracted many sitters.

When members of the Zhao family of wealthy merchants died in 1099 in the town of Baisha in Henan province's Yu county, a funerary artist pictured the husband and wife in their tomb facing each other across a table, each seated on a protruding-crestrail chair. Behind each chair is a wave-decorated screen. On the table are two cups and a ewer filled with wine that is ready to be enjoyed. Below the table, their feet rest on footrests.[2] Nine years later, in 1108, a very similar chair was buried in the mud when torrential waters flooded the town of Julu in Hebei province. It lay there until it was unearthed —along with a table—in 1926.[3]

Late-Ming woodblock prints, dating from six centuries later, attest to the durability of this basic design. In Ming illustrated dramas innumerable figures are seated on *kaobeiyi*. The illustrations also remind us that the beautifully grained wood and elegant lines of these chairs were not always visible. The chairs are often shown covered with a rectangular piece of fabric, leaving just the legs and rear stiles exposed. The chair covers on *kaobeiyi* are usually decorated with simple, repeated patterns— plum blossoms, bamboo leaves—with a frame of a different pattern around the edge.

This particular pair of *kaobeiyi* is distinguished by beautifully grained wood on the back splats and a subtle but creative deviation from the standard design. The artisan of this chair followed the basic construction of the *kaobeiyi*, but added a few varia-tions borrowed from other furniture types. His most striking alteration was making the legs and all other members below the seat frame square in section on what otherwise would be a round leg construction. In addition, instead of making a flat one- or three-piece framework for the openings between the legs and the seat frame, he made a humpback stretcher, following the traditional design line and adding two vertical braces to help support the seat frame. (Square-section members and a humpback stretcher also appear on a pair of armchairs with protruding crestrails, dated 1550–1600, in the Victoria and Albert Museum.[4]) The result is a very classic design with its own distinction.

Construction

A round-section, humpback crestrail protrudes over the two rear stiles. Single wide tenons on the top and bottom of the plain splat tenon into the crestrail and into the seat frame. The round-section rear stiles descend through the seat frame, under which they become square-section rear legs.

The seat is constructed of four mitered, through tenon frame members and has two transverse braces, curved front-to-back, below what were originally rattan and palm-fiber seats.

Below the seat are square-section, humpback stretchers that tenon into the legs. Two vertical braces on each stretcher butt tenon into the bottom of the seat frame and miter tenon into the stretcher.

The bottom stretchers all miter through tenon into the legs. They are arranged in graduated-height arrangement, known in Chinese as *bubugao*, a reference to rising in rank in officialdom.

Jin Ping Mei, Chongzhen (1628–1644) edition.

1. Tianran Chisou, p. 179.

2. Su Bai, *Baisha Song mu* (The Song Tombs of Baisha). Beijing: Wenwu Chubanshe, 1957, plate 22.

3. The chair is now at the Nanjing Museum, where I viewed it in April 1995. It is no longer standing as a chair, but is broken down to its parts of stretchers, stiles, and posts. This disassembled state allows observations of its mortise-and-tenon joinery. At several of the joints, holes for pins that reinforced the joints are clearly visible.

4. See Craig Clunas, *Chinese Furniture*. London: Victoria and Albert Museum, 1988, p. 18.

8. Pair of Armchairs with Protruding Crestrail, "Official's Hat Chair" [*fushouyi, guanmaoyi, sichutou*] 黃花梨 扶手椅，官帽椅，四出頭

47¼ in. (h) × 23 in. (w) × 17½ in. (d)

Huanghuali

Very quickly, the general walked out to the end of the boat, took a chair facing the bank and sat down. The mass of people howled as in a war cry, and Shu the Scholar was brought out. When he raised his head, all he saw was the general's knit eyebrows and his face full of murderous wrath.[1]

Along with the rounded-crestrail chair, the official's hat chair is one of the most stately forms of chair. Even when covered by a textile, the four protruding members are exposed, which visually invests the sitter with an extra measure of status.

Officials and some more-exalted members of society are often portrayed in woodblock prints and paintings seated in such chairs, which are known as *guanmaoyi* —official's hat chairs—for their visual resemblance to such dignitaries' hats, which had two silk protuberances on either side. Just as the addition of the back to a stool makes the side chair one step more comfortable and more proper, so the addition of arms also added further comfort and prestige.

Many of the early images of official's hat chairs depict monks and priests seated crosslegged, their feet up on the seat's surface area, which allowed enough room for the legs. By the early Song period, two sitting positions—legs pendant and legs folded—were acceptable on these chairs. The tenth-century woodblock landscape images that serve as frontispieces to an imperial commentary on the *Tripitaka,* now in the Harvard University Art Museum, show figures sitting in both types of position.[2]

Like side chairs and drum stools, official's hat chairs were often covered with textiles for increased comfort and adornment. Early woodblock prints and paintings, including the frontispiece mentioned above, also depict *guanmaoyi* with round-ended, woven-rattan or rush mats lain across the back and seat for extra cushioning. These mats are similar to the round woven mats originally used for sitting on the ground.

In the late Ming, the apparent plainness of this particular chair, and its lack of adornment, were as much an aesthetic statement as fine carving or gold dragons would have been. Many members of the

late-Ming elite strove for such simplicity. This pair of chairs relies solely on the subtly curving splats, stiles, and armrests and the finely grained wood to communicate an air of restrained elegance.

Construction

The protruding crestrail curves slightly upward at either end and is flattened at its center, where it meets the splat and where the neck of the sitter would rest. The S-curved splat, the sides of which have a quarter-round edge, is flush with the top of the crestrail and has a single wide tenon on top and bottom. The rear stiles miter tenon into the crestrail, the tenon pinned from the back. The stile follows the same S-shaped curve as the splat. The serpentine arms miter through tenon to the rear stiles and protrude beyond the front armposts. A central S-shaped side post supports the arm at its center, round tenoning into the underarm and seat frame. The front posts miter blind tenon into the arm.

The seat is constructed of four mitered, through tenon, frame members, and has two front-to-back, curved transverse braces below the rattan and palm-fiber seats. An exposed haunch adds greater support at all four mitered joins, keeping the two top surfaces flush.

The edge of the seat frame is a doubled, stepped molding. The front posts and rear stiles descend to become the legs of the chair. The inner surfaces of the legs are squared below the seat frame to add further support to the seat and to accept the three-sided interior frameworks. The two vertical sides of the framework meet the upper horizontal member with a half-lapped miter join. Only the front framework has a decorative bead and cusped outline. The other three sides are plain with a curvilinear, but not cusped, outline. The framework fits into a groove on the sides and tenons into the bottom stretcher.

The bottom stretchers all miter through tenon into the legs. They are arranged in the graduated-height arrangement known in Chinese as *bubugao*—rising step by step.

Small aprons further support the stretchers tenoning into the legs. The footrest on one of the chairs has been replaced, as has a vertical side member of

Xi Xiang Ji (Tale of the Western Chamber), 1614 Xiang Xue Ju edition.

the front framework and two aprons below the stretchers.

1. Li Yu, "Feng Xian Lou" (The Building of the First Offering), in *Shi Er Lou,* p. 296.

2. Max Loehr, *Chinese Landscape Woodcuts.* Cambridge, Mass.: Harvard University Press, 1968.

9. Armchair with Protruding Crestrail and Inward-curving Legs, "Official's Hat Chair" [*guanmaoyi, sichutou*] 黃花梨，官帽椅，四出頭

43 in. (h) × 24 in. (w) × 17 in. (d)
Huanghuali

Zhang Li led him through a large door, dragged out a chair and placed it at the front of the hall. He asked Xiao Lou to sit down. Then he passionately bowed down four times. When he was finished he asked Xiao Lou his name and his origins.[1]

This chair has a number of unusual and flamboyant variations that distinguish it from the standard protruding-crestrail chair. The most striking of these alterations is the inward-curving legs. Such legs are most often seen on couch-beds and occasionally on beds and stools. Woodblock prints from the late Ming period do depict chairs with such legs, but actual extant seventeenth-century examples are rare. A Qing-period rounded-crestrail chair at the Palace Museum in Beijing has curved legs but it sits on a *tuoni* (continuous floor stretcher).[2] The presence of curved legs throws off the standard chair form by not affording proper space for a footrest and bottom stretcher. The *tuoni* on the Palace Museum chair provides a footrest and also further restrains the legs from spreading outward, as do the lower stretchers on all chairs. Because this chair has neither a *tuoni* nor lower stretchers to reinforce its structure, giant's arm braces have been added, extending from the inside of the legs to the transverse braces below the seat. While giant's arm braces are common to tables and are occasionally seen on stools, they are rare on chairs.

The overall height of this chair is surprisingly low. The seat is 18¼ inches high, in comparison with the usual 20 inches. This chair may possibly have been placed upon a rectangular raised platform or stand. Such a platform, which can be seen in "Huan Cui Tang Yuan Jing Tu" (Scenes and Pictures of the Huan Cui Tang Garden), the Wanli reign period woodblock print at right, would have afforded the sitter a footrest, thus accommodating the Chinese predilection for keeping one's feet off the potentially cold ground. It would also elevate the sitter to a properly dignified height. While these platforms seem not to have survived in great quantity, they appear frequently in Wanli reign period wood-

block prints, such as in the "Lie Nu Zhuan." It is possible that certain objects now classified as *kang* tables are actually chair platforms. A lacquer throne chair at the Victoria and Albert Museum has curved legs and sits atop such a detachable platform with matching footstool.[3] If the chair included here once had a platform, it has been separated from it for some time since the worn feet testify to long contact with a harsh ground.

In addition to these structural variations, the artisan or chair designer chose to make members square that are usually round in section. The crestrail, the arms, the posts, and the stiles are all square in section, giving the chair a bolder and more muscular appearance. A Jiajing reign period carved-lacquer chair with a protruding crestrail as well as a waist (National History Museum, Beijing), like this chair, also has square-section members, as do a pair of protruding-crestrail chairs at the Victoria and Albert Museum.[4]

The exaggerated curled ends of this chair's protruding crestrail are reminders of an original source of the projecting upturned rail. Song imperial portraits depict the Emperor Taizu and the Empress Zhenzong sitting in chairs with protruding crestrails with ends of gold (or brass) sculpted into lively dragon heads.[5]

The scroll-like carving of the neckrest, which is echoed by the scrolling curls on the feet, is reminiscent of imitation scrolls seen painted on Kangxi era (1662–1722) porcelain. A similar neckrest can be seen on a late Ming–early Qing throne at the Chengde Summer Palace.[6] This detail suggests that the chair dates to the latter half of the seventeenth century, while it still retains the structure, style, and fine design of early seventeenth-century workmanship.

Construction
The square-sectioned crestrail, with a raised center section carved as if scrolling backward, and with slightly raised ends, protrudes beyond the rear stiles. These, in turn, curve forward as they descend and drop directly below the arm to the seat frame. At its top end, the S-curved splat has one long, continuous tenon, which fits into the crestrail; at its lower end, two

Huan Cui Tang Yuan Jing Tu (Scenes and Pictures of the Huan Cui Tang Garden), Wanli.

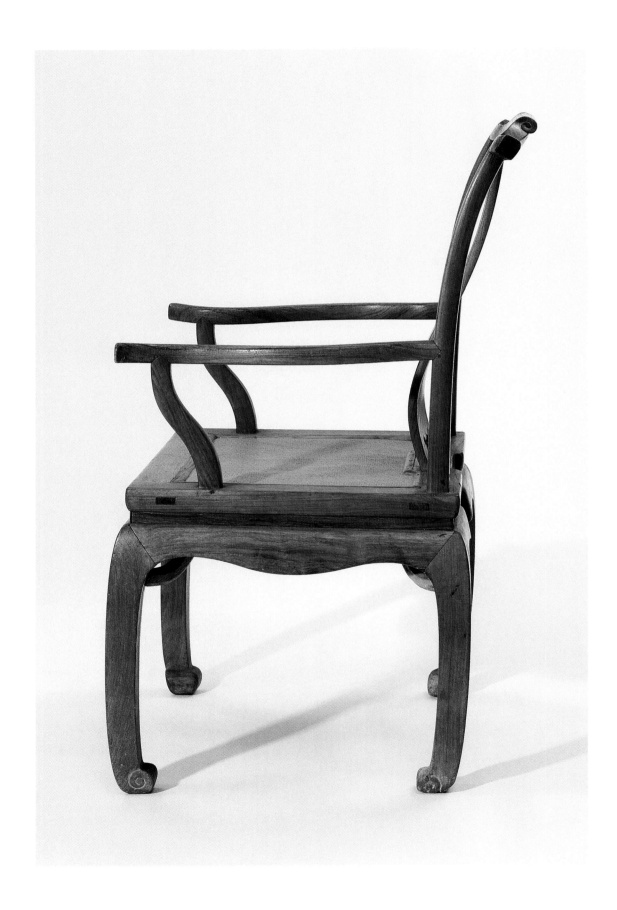

10. Armchair with Decorative Inlaid Splat, "Southern Official's Hat Chair" (set of four)
[*fushouyi, fangyi, nan guanmaoyi*] 黃花梨 扶手椅，方椅，南官帽椅
48 in. (h) × 23 in. (w) × 17 in. (d)

Huanghuali with mother-of-pearl, ebony, boxwood, and horn

tenons fit into the back seat frame member. The bottom, center section of the splat has a pierced, cusped outline with beading.

S-shaped arms of square section blind miter tenon into the rear stiles. The side posts also blind miter tenon into the arms and then descend backward in an S-shaped curve and tenon into the seat frame.

The seat frame is constructed of four mitered, through mortise-and-tenon members. The center section of the rear frame member indents toward the center of the seat, behind the splat, creating a reverse humpbacklike shape.

The rear stiles join the rear legs where they meet within the seat frame member, attaching to one another with a half-lapped, pinned scarf joint. Below the seat frame, two curved transverse braces tenon into the front and rear seat frame members. Giant's arm braces, each constructed of a single piece of elm wood, tenon into the inner corners of the legs and rest in slanted notches on the transverse braces, where they are nailed in place.

The waist, with mitered edges notched into the leg post, sits below the seat frame and atop the apron; it is held in place by a tapered dovetail key, which also goes through the apron.

The rear apron and rear waist follow the same contour as the seat's indented rear frame member. The aprons rest on and meet the legs in a mitered, lapped tenon.

The legs bulge outward and then curve back in, ending in scrolled hoof feet.

1. Bo Juyi (772–846), *The Cottage* (817). From Richard E. Strassberg, trans., *Inscribed Landscapes: Travel Writing from Imperial China.* Berkeley: University of California Press, 1994, p. 136.

2. Wang Shixiang, *Classic Chinese Furniture.* San Francisco: China Books and Periodicals, 1986, pp. 102–103.

3. Pictured in Michel Beurdeley, p. 126, and in Craig Clunas, *Chinese Furniture*, p. 32.

4. Craig Clunas, *Chinese Furniture*, p. 18.

5. *Masterpieces of Chinese Portrait Paintings in the National Palace Museum.* Taibei: National Palace Museum, 1970, plates 17 and 20.

6. Wang Shixiang, *Connoisseurship of Chinese Furniture.* Hong Kong: Joint Publishing, 1990, vol. 2, p. 60.

Recently I heard that someone in Beijing was selling a zitan *chair of excellent quality which was decorated with pearls, jade, and precious materials. A high official's son wanted to buy it for 120 liang of silver.*[1]

Adding to the already gracefully delineated crestrails, legs, and stiles of each chair, which together produce a very satisfying form, finely carved, multimaterial-inlaid designs adorn the back splats of these four chairs.

This multimaterial-inlay technique—seen in lacquer as well as in hardwood—is termed *bai bao qian* (one-hundred-treasure inlay) and dates back at least to the Tang period. An early example is the carved *zitan pipa* (lute) inlaid with mother-of-pearl and hardstone, which dates to the Tang and is stored in the Shoso-in in Nara, Japan. The striking technique continued to be used through the centuries, and the late Ming writer Wen Zhenheng mentions furniture with mother-of-pearl inlay several times. A Ming *zitan* box at the Palace Museum in Beijing, decorated with a mother-of-pearl and hardstone-inlay design of two birds on a branch, is a fine example of the technique.[2] As Wang Shixiang has noted, texts record the name Zhou Zhu as a craftsman who specialized in this technique.[3] The presence of an artisan's name within the world of furniture, which has so few names associated with its craft, demonstrates the high esteem in which pieces decorated in this manner were held. This is further borne out by an additional Ming text that notes a high price paid for a *zitan*-inlaid chair, which may be seen in the quote noted above by Wang Shizhen (1634–1711) in his book *Fen Gan Yu Hua* (After Sharing the Joy).

Images of birds and flowers, such as those on these chairs, had their first great wave of popularity during the Song period. Imperial patronage at that time particularly favored this theme. Emperor Song Huizong (ruled 1101–25) was a bird-and-flower painter himself. During the Yuan and Ming periods, landscape became the supreme motif of literati painters, but those in professional and more academic schools continued practicing the bird-and-flower tradition. The early Ming emperor, Xuanzong (ruled 1427–35), was also a

bird-and-flower painter. The motif was favored by many patrons, not only as a subject for their paintings but as decoration on objects as well. Ming porcelains often display birds and flowers. The woodblock-print painting manuals of the seventeenth century, among them *Shi Zhu Zhai Huapu* (Ten Bamboo Studio Painting Manual), *Jiezi Yuan Huazhuan* (Mustard Seed Garden Painting Manual), and *Gu Shi Huapu* (Gu Painting Manual), all included a series of bird-and-flower paintings for the beginning painter—or artisan—to study. The appearance and proliferation of these bird-and-flower images by means of woodblock prints may have aided the appearance of bird and flower motifs in the decorative arts.

In addition to their visual appeal, the presence of these birds carried auspicious meanings. Specific birds and flowers each expressed particular wishes. For instance, as seen here, the magpie and the plum blossom represent, in rebus form, the wish *xishangmeishao* (happiness up to one's eyebrows). *Bai tou fu gui* (white-head blessings and wealth) expresses the wish that a couple be together until their old age and live in luxury. This is conveyed with the image of a grackle (or grey starling), a white-headed bird known in Chinese as a *bai tou weng*, perched among peonies—the king of flowers.

The elaborate ornament on these chairs does not overwhelm their calm and elegant countenance. The decoration is well balanced with the large, handsome, and otherwise unadorned structure.

Construction

The crestrail of the chair caps over the rear stiles and is pipe joined to them by a long, blind square tenon at the top of the rear stile. At its center, the crestrail rolls backward in an exaggerated manner. The splat, which meets the crestrail flush, descends in an elongated S-shaped curve to the center of the rear member of the seat frame. Single, long, rectangular tenons, centered at the top and bottom of the splat, fit into the crestrail and the rear seat member. The rear stiles are not straight but instead curve gently backward toward the crestrail. They pass through the mitered seat frame, at which point their inner sides take on a square corner (known in

Chinese as *waiyuanlifang*—outer round, inner square) providing a step to support the seat frame. The serpentine arms meet the rear stiles with a stepped through tenon.

In the same manner as the crestrail meets the rear stiles, the arms meet the front stiles by capping over them in a pipe join. A tenon in the front post meets a mortise in the arm. S-shaped side posts, tapering at the top, fit into the seat frame with rectangular tenons and add extra support to the arm. The armposts do not descend straight down, but curve back in an S-curve toward the seat before penetrating it to become the front legs.

The seat frame is constructed of four mortised-and-tenoned members, all with molded, inward-slanting edges, and tenons extending through the two side members. The seat has two transverse braces, their tops scooped for more comfortable seating on the flexible rattan seat. Along the inner sides of each frame member is a rabbet for accepting the splines that cover the edges of the rattan seat.

The aprons on the front and side openings are flat across, with no beading or decorative outline. Each is composed of three half-lapped, mitered, joined members. The sides fit into the legs with tongue-and-groove joins, and tenon into the footrest. The back apron is made of a single piece of wood. It does not descend as far down as the rear stretcher, but tenons into the rear legs.

The side and front stretchers are all at the same height, joined to the legs with staggered mitered tenons. The tenons extending through to the front of the legs are covered by the ends of the footrest. Below each stretcher is a smaller, one-piece apron.

The side stretchers are flat on top and rounded on the sides. This edge is more pointed on two of the four chairs in this set. The rear stretcher is oval shaped and flat on top.

Shui Hu Zhuan (The Water Margin), Wanli Rong Yu Tang edition.

1. Wang Shizhen, *Fen Gan Yu Hua* (After Sharing the Joy). Trans. in Wang Shixiang, *Connoisseurship of Chinese Furniture,* vol. 1, p. 145.

2. Gu Gong Bowuyuan, *Gu Gong Bowuyuan Cang Gongyipin Xuan* (Selections of Arts and Crafts in the Palace Museum). Beijing: Wenwu Chubanshe, 1974, p. 51.

3. Wang Shixiang, *Connoisseurship of Chinese Furniture,* vol. 1, p. 145.

11. Round-back Chair [*quanyi, yuanyi*] 紫檀 圈椅，圓椅

41 in. (h) × 24½ in. (w) × 19¼ in. (d)
Zitan
Seventeenth–eighteenth century

Eunuch Sha winked at one of his servants, who substituted some drugged wine and filled the young man's cup with it. Not long after drinking it, Ruxiu began to grow limp. His head lolled forward and he slumped in the easy chair. He slept a sleep as sound as Chen Tuan's.[1]

The round-back chair, like the folding round-back chair, was a seat of honor. In addition, however, it could be used for casual sitting or as a dining chair. Ming woodblock prints depict high officials seated in these chairs greeting guests of lower rank, but in other contemporary illustrations, rowdy drinkers at an inn also sit on chairs of the same shape.

The Ming encyclopedia, the *San Cai Tu Hui,* captions an illustration of a chair of this form with the term *yuanyi,* a round chair. Qing imperial texts refer to the form as a *quanyi,* a circular chair, and that name is still used in Chinese today. The term *horseshoe chair*—or *horseshoe-back chair*—commonly used in the English language, is not a derivation of any Chinese word for this type of chair.

As with many other shaped formal chairs, the round-back chair is often pictured covered by sumptuous textiles, with only the outward-curving ends of the arms exposed.

Construction

The continuous rounded crestrail is composed of five curved sections joined together by half-lapped, pinned, scarf joints. The arm ends protrude over the front posts with an exaggerated outward curve.

The single-curve splat, with a half-round edge, tenons into the crestrail on top and into the back seat frame member. A carved, raised medallion decorates the splat.

The rear stiles blind miter tenon into the crestrail and are pinned. S-curve side posts with round tenons stretch between the crestrail and seat frame. The curved front posts meet the armrail with a single mitered tenon. A beaded and shaped spandrel sits in a groove on the front post and under the extended section of the crestrail to add support.

The seat frame is composed of four members joined by mitered through tenons, exposed on the sides. The two curved transverse braces below the seat frame tenon into the front and rear seat frame members.

The round front posts and rear stiles descend to become the legs of the chair. Below the seat frame, the outer surfaces of the legs remain round, but the inner surfaces become square to add further support to the seat and to accept the three-sided interior framework. The two vertical sides of the framework meet the upper horizontal member with a half-lapped, mitered join and tenon into the bottom stretcher. Only the front framework, with its cusped outline, has a raised decorative carving of scrolling vines across its horizontal member. The side frameworks are plain with a beading along their cusped outlines.

The bottom stretchers all are mitered through tenoned into the legs and are placed in the graduated-height arrangement known as *bubugao.* The footrest is covered in brass.

Small aprons further support the front and side stretchers tenoning into the legs.

Jin Ping Mei, Chongzhen edition.

1. Li Yu, "Cui Ya Lou" (The House of Gathered Refinements). Trans. by Patrick Hanan in *The Invention of Li Yu.* Cambridge, Mass.: Harvard University Press, 1988, p. 101.

12. Low-back Chair, "Rose Chair"
[*meigui yi, wenyi*] 黃花梨 玫瑰椅，文椅

40 in. (h) × 23 in. (w) × 18 in. (d)
Huanghuali

On my pillow the sound of the pine, at daybreak, whistles repeatedly,
In front of my window the plum and the bamboo compete with their purity and wonder.[1]

There were a pair of jet black satin shoes; a pair of scent bags with the drawnwork inscription: "In secret tryst a lover's vow, I'll follow you where'er you go"; and a pair of russet satin kneepads, the borders of which were decorated with a motif of pines, bamboos, and plum blossoms, the "three cold-weather friends."[2]

While simple, styled furniture developed its own timeless designs following the physical structures required by each form, more ornate furniture of the late Ming and early Qing displayed decorations that often paralleled the aesthetic tastes and interests of the time.

The botanical motif that covers the back and side panels of this chair—pine, bamboo, and plum blossom—was extremely popular during the Ming period. Known in Chinese as the "three friends of winter"—because the pine and the bamboo both stay green through the harsh months of winter, and the plum blossom flowers in February—this grouping came to represent the ability to survive during adversity and, in particular, to denote the ability of an official or scholar to maintain his gentlemanly spirit, even during a politically challenging regime. These three plants had long been favorite topics for literati. Song and Yuan poets, artists, and calligraphers were passionate about the bamboo, the pine, and the plum blossom, representing them individually or in pairs. But it was not until the Ming that the image of the three plants together became popular and earned their poetic appellation. The subject appeared not only in furniture carvings, but also on paintings, ceramics, and jade carvings as well as in lines of poetry and threads of textiles.

Several other extant pieces of sixteenth- and seventeenth-century furniture display carvings of the three friends of winter. The top of a low lacquer table, with an inscribed date of the Jiajing reign period, has an incised design of this motif (collection of Li

Wu Sao Ji, 1614 edition.

Yuguan, Tokyo).[3] A very expensive, mother-of-pearl-inlaid lacquer bed purchased for one of Ximen Qing's wives, Pan Jinlian, is described in chapter twenty-nine of the novel *Jin Ping Mei* as having three panels of the interior "comb backs" all decorated with "pine, bamboo, and plum blossom, the three friends of winter." As Craig Clunas has pointed out,[4] the presence of this motif on a woman's bed demonstrates how this theme, once in the domain of the literati, by the late Ming had become appropriated by more popular and more feminine patrons. In a similar vein, the artisan who designed illustrations to the *Wu Sao Ji*, published in 1614, chose to portray a female character reposing on a couch-bed, the back and side panels and the apron of which are decorated with pine trees and bamboo.

Construction

The straight crestrail curves down at the ends to cap onto the rear stiles with mortise-and-tenon pipe joins. A groove runs under the entire crestrail, along the inside of the rear stiles and along the top edges of a rail just above the seat frame, to hold a pierced, carved panel. On the front of the panel, raised, pierced carving is

enclosed within a beaded frame with cusped corners. The pierced panel is flat and undetailed on the back. The rail below the panel and above the seat frame tenons into the rear stiles, which have a slight taper.

Straight, round arms meet the rear stiles with mitered tenon joins and end by curving down to cap the front posts, again with mortise-and-tenon pipe joins.

Carved, pierced panels are placed within the opening between the arm and the seat. A groove that runs along the lower edge of the arm, along the front post and the rear stile, and in a rail that stretches between the front post and rear stile, just above the seat frame, holds the panel.

The seat is constructed of four mitered through tenon members, with tenons exposed only on the sides.

The round front posts and rear stiles extend through the seat to become legs, all of which, below the seat frame, become square on the inside and round on the outside.

Between the two front legs and on the sides are three-member frameworks joined by half-lapped, mitered joins and tenoning into the footrest. The front apron with cusped outline is decorated with a raised, scrolling vine and a raised beading on the edge.

The four lower stretchers between the legs are staggered in the *bubugao* fashion, the front stretcher being the lowest, the side stretchers of medium height, and the back stretcher the highest. This staggering prevents several mortise-and-tenon joins from being located at the same height and weakening the leg.

The side stretchers are rounded on their outer sides and flat on top, with plain, one-piece aprons below. The rear stretcher has no apron and is rounded on the outside but square on the top and interior.

1. Wei Guan (b. 1305) in *Quan Ming Shi* (The Complete Ming Poems). Shanghai: Guji Chubanshe, 1990, p. 540.

2. *Jin Ping Mei* (1618). In David Tod Roy, trans., *The Plum in the Golden Vase*. Princeton, New Jersey: Princeton University Press, 1993, chapter 8, p. 160.

3. Illustrated in Beurdeley, p. 100.

4. Craig Clunas, "The Novel *Jin Ping Mei* as a Source for the Study of Ming Furniture," *Orientations* 1/92, pp. 60–68.

13. Daybed [*ta*] 核桃木 榻

20½ in. (h) × 71¼ in. (w) × 34 in. (d)
Walnut
Eighteenth century

Bamboo bed, rattan pillow,
    bean vines encircle the cabinet—
I loosen my sash, and lie down for an idle nap
    after the noon meal.
When the strength of the wine overcomes me,
    I travel within the borders of dreams.
Suddenly, the book I was holding in my hand drops.[1]

A painting attributed to the sixteenth-century artist Qiu Ying (1522–60) portrays a scholar playing his *qin* (zither), seated on a bamboo daybed, a pile of books and a bundle of scrolls beside him.[2]

Bamboo was favored both as a construction material and an aesthetic motif. For the less wealthy, bamboo was a readily available material—inexpensive and plentiful as well as pliable and sturdy. For the literati as well as Buddhists and Taoists, bamboo symbolized humbleness and represented a return to nature and its forms. Paintings from the Song and before depict Buddhist devotees seated in bamboo chairs. In a Lu Lengjia (active 730–60) painting depicting the Six Esteemed Ones (Palace Museum Collection, Beijing), a Buddhist figure is shown seated on a large bamboo official's hat chair with a matching footstool.[3] The appeal of bamboo continued through the Qing—a Yongzheng reign period (1722–35) portrait of a palace girl depicts her on an elegant fan-shaped, speckled bamboo chair.[4]

Bamboo furniture was popular and comfortable, but it was not as durable or as luxurious as fine hardwood furniture. With imitation-bamboo furnishings, the owner could express the humbleness of a refined gentleman, while maintaining the dignity of a man of status. In addition, he could impress his friends with the realistic carving skills of his carpenter. Several other extant pieces of imitation bamboo—including an early Qing rounded-crestrail chair (Nelson-Atkins Museum of Art, Kansas City) and an early Qing *kang* table (Central Academy of Arts and Crafts, Beijing)[5]—demonstrate the penchant for this style. Imitation bamboo also extended to other materials. The handles and edge ornaments of an early Qing bronze vase (Clague collection, Phoenix, Arizona), for example, were formed to imitate bamboo stalks.[6]

In China, trompe-l'oeil was popular not only in wood but in porcelain as well, particularly in the eighteenth century. During the Yongzheng and Qianlong reign periods, brushpots, vases, and bowls were finely crafted out of porcelain, perfectly mimicking wood, lacquer, and bronze. Slight irregularities were often added to further the semblance of the imitated material. To enhance the likeness of bamboo in the carving of this daybed, for instance, the carpenter made the space between the growth rings on the legs successively larger, as they would be on an actual bamboo stalk.

Construction

The top bedframe is constructed of four frame members with mitered blind mortise-and-tenon joins. A straight stretcher abuts the framework directly below it, joining to the legs with a rounded, lapped wrapping around the leg, and a blind tenon. Four corner-crossing, blind mortise-and-tenoned braces and two large, scooped transverse braces are below the palm and rattan coverings. The palm is attached at a lower point of the inward-slanting frame member, while the rattan is woven into a groove closer to the outside of the frame. Humpback stretchers attach to the legs by rounded, lapped joints with blind tenons. Pairs of vertical braces are placed between the upper and lower stretchers. The top tenon of these braces passes through the upper stretcher and penetrates the top frame member, locking down the top frame. At the center of each humpback stretcher is an additional decorative pierced brace. At either end of the long sides are additional relief-carved, lobe-shaped braces. All joints are reinforced with square wooden pegs. The spaces between the growth rings on the carving imitating bamboo increase as they rise to the top of the leg giving the impression of a tapered leg.

Feng Yue Zheng Qi, 1620 edition.

1. "Miscellaneous Poems from My Studio on an Autumn Day," by Zhu Yunming (1461–1527). From Wang Xinzhan, ed., *Zhu Zhishan Shi Wenji* (A Collection of Zhu Zhishan Poetry). Shanghai: Guangyi Shuju, 1936, p. 101.

2. Published in Eli Lancman, *Chinese Portraiture.* Tokyo: Tuttle, 1966, p. 137.

3. Published in *Gugong Bowuyuan Canghua Ji* (Collected Paintings in the Palace Museum). Beijing: Renmin Meishu Chubanshe, 1978, vol. 1, pp. 58–69.

4. Published in *Qingdai Gongting Hui Hua* (Qing Palace Painting). Beijing: Wenwu, 1993, p. 97.

5. Wang Shixiang, *Connoisseurship of Chinese Furniture,* vol. 2, p. 68.

6. Robert Mowry, *China's Renaissance in Bronze.* Phoenix, Arizona: Phoenix Art Museum, 1993, p. 157.

14. Couch-bed [*ta, luohanchuang*][1] 黃花梨 榻，羅漢床

32½ in. (h) × 82⅜ in. (w) × 41½ in. (d)
Huanghuali

It was only on the first floor that, because he was extremely hospitable and because people often came from a distance to visit him, he placed a couch [ta] in the center of the room, and put up a plaque saying "To Be a Disciple of People."[2]

Early in Chinese history, during the Shang period (sixteenth–eleventh centuries B.C.), people sat or kneeled on mats laid on the ground. Over the next three millennia, sitting postures gradually changed and by the Song many people were sitting on chairs, their legs pendant. The *ta* is a uniquely Chinese form that allows one to sit either with legs pendant or in the more ancient mat posture, with legs and feet up on the sitting surface. Woodblock prints and paintings of the Ming period attest to the variety of postures that this furniture type allowed.

An illustration from *Jin Ping Mei* portrays Ximen Qing watching his maids make tea with boiled water made from freshly fallen snow. He sits on a simple three-panel couch-bed, which is very similar to this one, with one leg folded, knee up, and the other folded down on the surface of the bed.[3] Other contemporary illustrations show figures sitting at the edge of the couch-bed, their legs pendant, or more casually reclined, their legs completely stretched out on the couch's surface.

Couch-beds were used in formal and semi-formal rooms. Unlike a canopy bed, a host may sit on a couch-bed to receive guests formally, as is demonstrated by the quotation above. But, as illustrations in *Jin Ping Mei* also reveal, napping and love-making also happened on the woven rattan surfaces of these couch beds.

The simple design of this bed—with its few subtle design elements: the back panel higher than the sides, which Ming connoisseurs of furniture proclaimed to be more elegant; the curved step at the ends of the back panel and the front of the side panels; and the handsomely shaped legs and waist—allows the stunning quality of the wood and its grain to stand out. In *Ge Gu Yao Lun* (Essential Criteria of Antiquities), the author Cao Zhao states that *huali* "with ghost face markings is very pleasing."[4] The knots in the grain on the back panel of this couch-bed provide an example of such a striking "ghost face."

Construction

The three rectangular railings with indented corners are solid boards, all of which seem to have been cut from the same tree as the grain and knot formations relate to each other, confirming the couch-bed's authenticity and adding to its visual splendor.

At either end, the rear railing has caps attached by through tenons to prevent exposing the end grain and to make a stronger joint for the side railings. Three tenons are fitted into the bottom of the railing to join it to the bedframe. The tenons on the side railings fit into sliding, locking mortises on the endcaps of the rear railing, and tenon into the side members of the bedframe.

The bedframe is constructed of four mitered through tenon frame members, the tenons exposed only on the sides. Below the frame are four front-to-back transverse braces now attached to boards by sliding dovetails in grooves. The boards are later substitutes for the original palm-fiber and rattan seat. Plugged holes for the fibers and rattan are visible on the underside of the seat frame members.

Below the frame, the waist and apron are comprised of a single piece of wood. The mitered, rounded horse-hoof-footed legs have a tapered dovetail wedge that the apron slides over and locks into with through-dovetail housing. Two sliding keys dovetail onto the front apron, and one onto the rear apron, both of which lock the aprons onto the frame.

Characters written in ink on the legs and apron designate the right, left, front, and rear corner members.

Jin Ping Mei, Chongzhen edition.

3. *Jin Ping Mei Chatu Ji* (A Collection of Jin Ping Mei Illustrations). Guangxi: Guangxi Meishu Chubanshe, 1993, p. 45.

4. Translated from a facsimile of the 1388 text published in Sir Percival David, *Chinese Connoisseurship: The Ko Ku Yao Lun.* New York: Praeger, 1971.

1. The term *luohanchuang* has recently been associated with this form of furniture and, according to Wang Shixiang, is used by northern cabinetmakers. Since no Ming texts employ the words *luohan* and *chuang* together, I have chosen to avoid its use. The word *ta*, however, does appear quite often. Though by dictionary definition *ta* is a platform without rails, the *San Cai Tu Hui* illustrates *ta* with a three-railed platform couch. For the English translation I have elected the term *couch-bed*, first suggested by Sarah Handler, to refer to this type of furniture as it best describes its shape and multiple uses.

2. Li Yu (1611–80), "San Yu Lou" (The Building of the Three Teachers), in *Shi Er Lou*, p. 59.

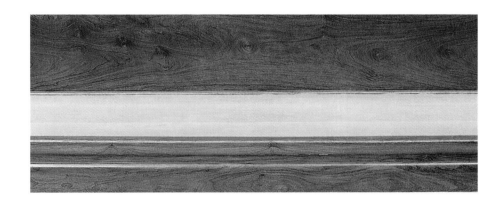

15. Couch-bed with Pierced, Carved Railings [*ta, luohanchuang*] 黃花梨 榻，羅漢床

32 in. (h) × 82 in. (w) × 41 in. (d)
Huanghuali

Among the clouds a pair of phoenixes call
Going out and returning to the city.[1]

The basic outline of this *ta* resembles that in the previous entry, but the elaborate openwork carving suggests a radically different taste. The preference of the literati for simple design became popular even among the nonliterati elite during the seventeenth century. However there were still many patrons who appreciated beautiful displays of fine carving and all they implied. Moreover, decorated rails around a couch-bed are reminders that the form probably developed from the ancient custom of sitting on mats or low platforms surrounded on three sides by elegantly adorned screens, such as seen on a Han tomb mural in Liaoning.

The appearance of fully and finely carved furniture in the seventeenth century was neither sudden nor unanticipated. A number of earlier precedents mark a pathway leading to these pieces. Dated carved cinnabar-lacquer furniture, such as the Xuande reign period (1426–35) coffer at the Victoria and Albert Museum, demonstrate an early taste for fully ornamented furnishings.[2] A small Yuan-period ceramic throne in the Beijing Palace Museum collection also displays lavish adornment. The back rail is constructed of three panels and each side is a single panel, all five of which are decorated to resemble carvings of flowers and leaves on vines. The panels all have cusped corners echoing the indented corners of this couch-bed.

The most remarkable feature of this couch-bed is the fine openwork carving on the rails. The center panel of the back rail, depicting two phoenixes, is the most outstanding of the seven panels and was most likely carved by a different hand than the one that executed the smaller panels. The leaves on this panel curl with a flourish at their ends and the birds are delineated in an extremely naturalistic manner. While the carving hand may have changed —perhaps an apprentice was assigned the smaller panels—the bird motif of the carving is continuous across the seven panels.

Since as early as the Shang and Zhou periods, the appearance of specific birds, flowers, and other creatures have been regarded as auspicious omens in China. The sculpting, carving, drawing, or even embroidering of their images on objects subsequently came to communicate a wish for all that actual appearances of those creatures promised.

The carved central panel on the back rail depicts two phoenixes, portrayed with such care that even their individual feathers are sculpted. The phoenix (*fenghuang*) is a mythical fowl, considered the king of all birds, and discussed in Chinese texts as early as twenty-five hundred years ago. It is said to have the head of a chicken, the neck of a snake, the jaws of a swallow, the back of a tortoise, the tail of a fish, and feathers of five colors. The appearance of a phoenix at the time of Confucius was believed to signify Heaven's approval of a ruler and peace in the land. Through the centuries, both the phoenix's image and its intended symbolism has undergone many transformations. In popular Chinese imagery a pair of phoenixes represents marital bliss. According to Wolfram Eberhard, two phoenixes with a blossom between them expresses "connubial intercourse."[3]

The other six panels in the railings around the bed depict pairs of nonmythical birds surrounding flowers. Each bird species symbolizes specific desired joys: the magpie and mandarin ducks, for instance, both denote marital happiness. The multiplicity of such motifs suggests that this piece may have been part of a dowry. A carved lacquer couch-bed in the Philadelphia Museum of Art has seven panels on its railings carved with similar bird and plant groupings that include a phoenix on the central, largest panel.

If one crawls under this piece of furniture an interesting linguistic detail is revealed. A two-character ink inscription— *luo han*—is written on one of the side frame members. Wang Shixiang has remarked that the term *luohanchuang* was current among northern carpenters when denoting this type of furniture, though no known Ming text employs the word. The presence of the characters on this piece— whether written by the original carpenter or a later restorer (see below)—confirms the application of the term.

Construction

Three rectangular railings, all with indented corners, form the back and two sides of this couch-bed. The back railing is higher than the two side railings, which consist of four-sided frames with mitered through tenon corners, within which float pierced, carved panels. The top frame member of the rear railing pipe joins to the side frame members with tenons exposed on the top. Additional frame members separate the panels within each railing, and the panels float within grooves on the frame members. The rear railing has three floating panels, while the two side railings each have two.

Four tenons are fitted into the bottom of the rear railing to join it to the bedframe. The tenons on the side railings fit into sliding, locking mortises on the end frame members of the rear railing, and tenon into the side members of the bedframe.

The bedframe is constructed of four frame members with mitered through tenons that are exposed only on the sides. Below the frame and palm matting are four curved, front-to-back transverse braces.

Below the frame, the waist and apron comprise a single piece of wood. The aprons on all four sides have cusped outlines, relief carving, and beaded edges. Cabriole legs have tapered, dovetail wedges over which the apron slides and into which it locks with through dovetail housing.

1. Wang Jian (c. 767–c. 830).

2. Reproduced in Craig Clunas, *Chinese Furniture*, p. 79.

3. Wolfram Eberhard, *A Dictionary of Chinese Symbols*. London: Routledge, 1986, p. 236.

16. Canopy Bed [*jiazi chuang*] 黃花梨 架子床

94½ in. (h) × 88¼ in. (w) × 61¾ in. (d)

Huanghuali

The old lady called out to them "Old Wu is coming!" The younger woman was in the room, her hands and legs already in nonstop action. She dashed up to block the door. Ximen Qing meanwhile slid under the bed to hide.[1]

The group of people went to the door of the room, pushed it open and looked in. On the bed hung curtains, there were chests and trunks, and sitting on the bed a young woman, wearing white and looking pure and beautiful as a flower and as jade. They all looked at her, but none dared move forward. One remarked: "I'm not sure if she is a god or ghost."[2]

Of the many years in a person's life, half are passed in the daytime and half are passed at nighttime. The daytime is spent either in halls or inner chambers or on boats or in vehicles, never in one specific place. But for the nighttime, the only location is the bed. A bed is the object with which we share half of our lives…so the relationship between a person and a bed is most intimate. Whenever I move to a new place, I first install a bed to sleep, then I take care of other things….One should treat a bed as one does a wife. If I don't have enough money to build a new bed, I still put all my efforts into decorating the bed and the bed curtains.[3]

In terms of decoration, the canopy bed was one of the most celebrated pieces of furniture in a household. After all, it was not only a place to rest, but also a place to frolic and, most importantly, the place where future heirs to the clan were conceived and born. It was also a convenient object under which characters in late-Ming fiction occasionally hid from jealous husbands. Or, as one distressed character in a Ming short story discovered, the top beam of her bed, with a hemp cord looped around it, became a helpful piece of equipment in her suicide attempt to protest an arranged marriage.[4]

The bed was the prime object a woman brought with her in her dowry. In *Jin Ping Mei*, the great erotic novel of the late Ming period, matchmakers brag about beds owned by potential brides, and wives bicker for finer beds than their rivals.

Most of these beds are described as lacquer—polychrome, or black with gold decorations, or inlaid with mother-of-pearl—alcove beds. The bed was one of the few items that remained in the woman's possession even after her marriage into her husband's family home. And, as Craig Clunas has noted, should the marriage be terminated, the bed still belonged to the wife.[5] The husband would visit a wife (and often he had several) in her quarters, and in her bed, for an evening, but the bed belonged to the woman.

On account of the woman's title to a bed, canopy beds frequently were more elaborately carved than, for instance, an austerely simple painting table in a man's study. When offering his opinion on the decoration of a man's bedroom, the Ming aesthete Wen Zhenheng advises keeping the atmosphere simple and plain, for too much prettiness would suggest a woman's room.[6]

The pierced carving on this bed is a repeated pattern of dragons. The archaistic style in which these fantastic and benevolent mythical creatures are depicted is reminiscent of the surface decoration of Zhou bronze vessels and was a style that became particularly popular in the second half of the seventeenth century.

Not all people in China spent their nights on six-poster canopy beds. In northern China, many activities—including eating and working as well as sleeping—took place on the *kang*, a large, elevated, brick platform heated by flues from within. As is demonstrated by bedroom descriptions in *Jin Ping Mei*, many households incorporated both *kang* and beds.

Construction

A framed, multiboard panel, with two battens crossing it and joined to the boards by sliding dovetails, forms the canopy cover of this bed. The frame is supported by the four corner posts, which butt tenon into its corners. Just below the canopy, on all four sides, are framed ornamental rails, which tenon into the canopy frame members and slide tenon into the posts. The front and rear rails each have three pierced, carved, floating lattice panels, separated by vertical dividers tenoned into the horizontal members, while the side rails each have two floating panels. The frame members

Xi Xiang Ji (Tale of the Western Chamber), Xiang Xue Ju edition, 1614.

are joined at their top corners with lapped mortise-and-tenon joins, their vertical side members descending below the lower horizontal frame members. Carved, pierced spandrels tenoned into this side and the lower frame member add support to the structure. The lattice sits in grooves on the frame members of the rails. At the front, the top rail is also supported by two additional, shorter, secondary posts that tenon into the bed frame. A humpback-shaped, carved, pierced spandrel stretches between each of the corner posts and the secondary posts, and two other triangular spandrels stretch between the secondary posts and the lower frame member of the top rail.

Between the posts, resting on the bed frame, are five railings—one in the back, one on either side, and two short ones between each of the front secondary posts and their respective, neighboring front corner posts. These railings tenon into the posts and bedframe. Each railing is constructed of a frame, with frame members joined by mitered through tenons. The upper corners of the frame are rounded. Below the top frame member are round, pierced, carved support braces

17. Painting Table [hua an]
黃花梨　畫案
33⅜ in. (h) × 82⅝ in. (w) × 41 in. (d)
Huanghuali and burl

On a cold night, sleep is very sweet. I woke in the middle of the night, my mind clear and untroubled, and as I was unable to go to sleep again, I put on my clothes and sat facing my flickering lamp. On the table [an] were a few sets of books in their wrappings. I chose a volume at random and began to read but, tiring, I put down the book and sat calmly doing nothing.[1]

The simple, elegant form of what has come to be known as the "standard" table[2]—typified by circular section, recessed legs, a flat, undecorated apron, short plain spandrels, and single or double side stretchers—was created in a wide variety of sizes, materials, and proportions for as wide a variety of uses. Woodblock prints portray this table form in the village inns as well as the halls of lofty scholars and officials. In an illustration from the Wanli reign period version of the novel *Shui Hu Zhuan* (The Water Margin), diners at a roadside inn have just risen from their meal of dumplings filled with human meat; the meal had been served on a large standard table. In the background, behind a door, a victim-to-be is laid out on a longer and narrower table of the same design. Undoubtedly, tables in such humble surroundings were made of soft and less-expensive woods. A table of precisely the same form is used as a desk—with brushes, books, inkstone, and brushwasher upon it—in an intimate tryst scene in a late-Ming illustration for *Xi Xiang Ji* (Tale of the Western Chamber). Here, the young scholar Zhang Gong chats with his aristocratic girlfriend Ying Ying.

The popularity of the standard table form was not only in the imagination of the woodblock designers. Tables of this form, constructed of less-expensive materials such as elm, pine, and lacquered softwoods, are still commonly seen in rural China today. Likewise, numerous beautifully crafted Ming *huanghuali*, and even *zitan*, examples are extant in Western and Chinese furniture collections.

That the simple shape was one favored by the elite of late-Ming China is confirmed by the inscription on a *huanghuali*

four frame members mitered with through mortise-and-tenons, the tenons exposed only on the sides. Below the frame are two curved, front-to-back transverse braces, two straight, front-to-back transverse braces toward the edge, and two additional shorter braces stretching between these straight braces and the side frame members.

Below the frame, the waist and apron are composed of one piece of wood. The serpentine-shaped legs have a tapered dovetail wedge that the ornamented and cusped-outline aprons slide over and lock into with through-dovetail housing. On the apron, two facing dragons, a *taotie*-like image between them, are carved in relief. The feet are distinguished by leaf ornaments on their exterior corners, and by low, round lobes on their interior surfaces.

1. *Shui Hu Zhuan*, p. 396.

2. "Bai Niangzi Yong Zhen Leifeng Ta" (The White Woman Forever Subdued in Leifeng Pagoda). In Hu Shibao, ed., *Gudai Baihua Duanpian Xiaoshuo Xuan* (Selections of Ancient Vernacular Short Stories). Beijing: Zhongguo Qingnian Chubanshe, 1962, p. 187.

3. Li Yu, "Chuang Zhang" (Beds and Bed Curtains), in *Xian Qing Ou Ji* (Casual Notes Written in Idleness). Hangzhou: Zhejiang Guji Chubanshe, 1985, p. 191.

4. Tianran Chisou, p. 30.

5. Clunas, *Chinese Furniture*, p. 94.

6. Craig Clunas, *Superfluous Things*. Urbana: University of Illinois Press, 1991, p. 54.

that tenon into the top frame member above and into an additional crossmember below. This additional crossmember mitered tenons into either side frame member. Carved, pierced panels float within the areas created by the bottom frame member, the two side members, and the additional crossmember. Long tenons on the sides of these panels fit into grooves on the side frame members, and additional small tenons join the panel to the upper and lower frame members.

The bedframe that supports this complex but stable canopy is constructed of

Xi Xiang Ji (Tale of the Western Chamber), Wanli edition.

table of this form (originally from Suzhou; now in the Nanjing Museum). The inscription, written in small seal script by the original owner, reads: "The materials are beautiful and solid, the craftsmanship is plain and lovely. If it is only for leaning on, it will allow me leisure for one hundred years. A day in the *yiwei* year of the Wanli reign [1595] signed the elder Chong An."[3]

This example of a standard table—which, like the inscribed table, originated in the southern Jiangsu region—is distinguished by its massive size, its beautiful *huanghuali* timbers, and the use of beautifully mottled burl wood for its top. Burl, like root wood and rocks, expressed the interest in nature and natural formations. Such large expanses of root were rare and treasured. Wang Zuo in his 1459 commentary on Cao Zhao's 1387 book *Ge Gu Yao Lun*, noted "Recently a Secretary on the Board of Revenue, He Shixun of Xuzhou, gave [me] a tabletop made of grape-faced

[wood], making it extremely beautiful. The wood is said to be the root of a thousand-year-old tree."[4]

The carpenter's extra care in placing the two burl panels in this table provides evidence of his skill and of the importance of this piece. Instead of merely cutting square-cornered panels, he created rounded edges for the burl and carved away matching rounded voids in the frame members.

Construction

The tabletop is constructed of four members joined by mitered blind tenons surrounding two burl-wood floating panels with rounded corners. Below the panels, five battens blind tenon into the long frame members and dovetail into sliding dovetail slots on the floating panels. Two further, thinner battens cross the length of the table, crossing under the long battens. There are no grooves on the frame mem-

18. Side Table with Recessed Legs [*pingtou an*] 漆 平頭案

33 in. (h) × 72 in. (w) × 28 in. (d)
Pine with polychrome lacquer
Seventeenth century

The Chen family sent Auntie Wen to announce that they would like to have his daughter, Ximen Dajie, carried across their threshold in marriage on the twelfth day of the sixth month. Ximen Qing found himself so "pushed and pressured" that he was unable to procure a bed for his daughter's trousseau in time for the occasion and had to supply her with one of the gilt-lacquer Nanjing alcove beds that had formed part of Meng Yü-lou's dowry.[1]

Since as early as the Shang and Zhou periods, lacquer has supplied an efficient as well as decorative covering for wooden surfaces in China. Once hardened, the lacquer—which is made from the resin of the lacquer tree, a type of sumac—becomes a water-resistant layer and a luxurious, glossy surface. The substance may also be mixed with mineral colors, such as cinnabar, to yield an array of colors. The corner and everted flange of a Han-period table, excavated in North Korea but probably manufactured in Sichuan, exhibits a green, yellow, red, and black geometric design.[2]

By the late Ming, a great variety of lacquering techniques had been developed to create an array of splendid surfaces on furniture. Lacquer is applied in multiple layers to create a thick and impenetrable surface. Lacquer artisans would carve into this surface to produce elaborate designs with depth. Black lacquer was often inlaid with mother-of-pearl or other precious materials for a striking affect, or dusted with powdered mica. The technique exhibited here, which is called *tian cai* (filling with color), was developed in the late-fifteenth or early sixteenth century. After several coats of the orange-red base lacquer has been applied and dried, the artisan carves his designs into the lacquer. Then the thin lines are filled with colors and frequently, in addition, with gold. During the early and middle Ming period, lacquered furniture was considered the most opulent on the market. It is significant that names of lacquer artisans are recorded in Ming texts, but the name of only one furniture maker of the Ming period has come to light in the many writings from that period.[3] It was not until the increase in imported hardwoods, such as *huali* and *zitan,* in the late

bers or long tenons on the panels to hold the panels in place. Instead, they sit in a rabbet cut out on the inside edges of the four frame members.

Massive round legs double blind tenon into the tabletop. A pair of oval-shaped stretchers blind tenon into the legs on either short end of the table. The front aprons and spandrels supporting the top frame on either side of the table are each constructed of seven pieces. The descending sections of the aprons, on either side of the legs, are joined to the horizontal sections by a half-lapped miter join and notch into a groove on the legs. The Wanli-dated table at the Nanjing Museum has the same apron construction. End aprons attach to the front aprons with mitered joins at each end. Original black lacquer, which is cracked in spots, covers the entire underside of the table.

1. Shen Zhou (1427–1509), partial inscription on the painting entitled *Night Vigil,* dated the fifteenth day of the seventh month in the year equivalent to 1492. Translation based on that in James Cahill's *Parting at the Shore* (New York: Weatherhill, 1978, p. 90). In the painting, the artist depicts himself seated on a low platform, staring out at the evening; the table, with the lamp and books, are off to

his side, and the table's surface is far above him. It is interesting that he refers to the table as an *an,* which is the word usually used for a table with recessed legs. The table in the painting, however, is corner-legged, suggesting that the words were employed interchangeably.

2. Sarah Handler, "Pieces in Context: An Approach to the Study of Chinese Furniture," Ph.D. diss., University of Kansas, 1983, p. 62.

3. *Nanjing Bowuyuan Cang Bao Lu* (Treasures of the Nanjing Museum Collection). Shanghai: San Lian Shudian, 1992, pp. 227–28.

4. Translation from David, *Chinese Connoisseurship,* p. 155.

Xi Xiang Ji (Tale of the Western Chamber), Xiang Xue Ju edition, 1614.

Ming, that any other furniture came to compete with lacquer for creating an impression of status.

The fondness in the seventeenth century for the simple, nonwaisted, standard table form is evident in this deluxe painted-lacquer version of the table. While the patrons desired a conspicuous and luxurious surface for this table, they chose the simple and restrained structure as a balancing foundation.

Peonies accompanied by a few butterflies flitting about in the air decorate the top surface of the table. A Taihu stone in front of the peony bush determines the ground plane, which indicates that the table was intended to be placed against a wall and viewed only from one specific side. The peony represents marital and sexual bliss but, more importantly, it is also considered the king of flowers and therefore is a symbol of high rank and wealth.

Construction
The basic construction of this table follows the "standard table" structure (as in cat. 17). The top consists of a frame of four mitered, mortise-and-tenon-joined members with a central, floating panel. A *lan-shuixian* (water-restraining line) rims the entire top surface. Below, adding support to the floating panel, are four battens that blind tenon into the frame. Original lac-

quering over ramie covers the bottom of the tabletop. Circular-section recessed legs through tenon into the frame members of the tabletop.

Cracks in the lacquer make it apparent that the aprons cross through the legs in an elongated bridle joint. The end apron below the tabletop, unlike end aprons on most noncollapsing tables, does not meet the apron in a mitered or dovetailed joint. Instead it overlaps and extends beyond the longer aprons in both the front and back. Though the joinery is hidden below the lacquer surface, one may safely surmise that the sliding dovetails on the longer aprons slip into grooves on the end aprons.

Between the circular-section legs at either end are two circular-section stretchers. The legs continue straight down, with a slight splay, and end in brass coverings.

1. *Jin Ping Mei* (based on Roy trans.), p. 147.

2. In the Harvard University Art Museum Collection. Other similar Han lacquer furnishings, found in Lolang, North Korea, and presently in the Archaeology Museum of the Democratic People's Republic of Korea, Pyongyang, are discussed in Sarah Handler, "The Korean and Chinese Furniture Traditions" (*Journal of the Classical Chinese Furniture Society*, vol. 4, no. 4 (Autumn 1994), pp. 45–57).

3. Liu Jingzhi is described with four words under the section heading *Great Craftsman*: "Skilled Hand in Small Wood" [i.e., furniture making]. Zhou Hui, *Jinling Suo Shi* (Details of Nanjing), 1610. Reprint. Shanghai: Wenxue Guji Kanxing Chubanshe, 1955, vol. 1, p. 187.

19. Long Table with Everted Flanges [*yanji, qiaotou an*] 黃花梨 翹頭案

34 in. (h) × 126 in. (w) × 24 in. (d)
Huanghuali

Xiao Jiang and Bian together knelt down before the table [an zhuo] to listen to the official make the settlement. The magistrate slammed the table and flying into a rage said: "The two of you, man and wife, don't have an ounce of propriety, using your daughter's whole life as if it were a matter of watching a play. Since you are planning to marry her off, everyone should discuss the matter, to see if the daughter and the son-in-law are compatible. Why should you match this kind of daughter to that kind of son-in-law!"[1]

Ming woodblock prints of shrines and temples, as well as walks through such consecrated spaces today, reveal large tables with everted flanges, exaggerated cabriole legs, and deep cusped aprons positioned with incense and offerings before images of deities. The term *altar table* is often used in the English language when referring to any rectangular table with everted flanges. That word, however, is misleading.

A review of woodblock prints demonstrates that tables with these appendages were not necessarily always used in the capacity of worship. An illustrated scene from chapter 13 of the Ming novel *Xin Lie Guo Zhi* shows an official seated with his meal on a *pingtou* (flat-ended) *an* (table), and, to his side, a larger *qiaotou an* (everted-end table) with carved designs on the two panels between the foot bases. Upon it are placed books, a bundle of scrolls, an unidentifiable object, and a tiered box with a handle. Beside the table is a drum stool, indicating that someone may have been sitting at the table inspecting the objects. An illustration from chapter 46 of a Wanli edition of *Shui Hu Zhuan* (The Water Margin) depicts an officiator seated on a rounded-crestrail chair with footrest, behind a table with everted flanges; two attendants, one on either side, hold fans. It is apparent from these images and many others that, during the late Ming period, tables with everted flanges were being used for a variety of purposes and not solely for worship.

Like the crestrail ends of a protruding-crestrail chair, and the outward-curling arms of the round-back chair, everted flanges on tables seem to be a mark of

status and power. They literally stand out and draw attention to themselves. It is possibly this aesthetic—and the presence of flanges on altar tables in temples—that earned them their religious association.

The flange on the table, like protruding and, often, upturned crestrails on chairs, may have been borrowed from architectural elements. Since at least the Han period (206 B.C.–220 A.D.), roof design of domestic houses as well religious and government buildings have included the *chi wei* (upturned fish tails or dragon heads) at either end of the roof's ridge, and *fei yan* (upturned and extended eaves) at the roof's corners. These protruding elements were integral to Chinese architecture and can be seen in Han pottery tomb houses as well as in twentieth-century rural homes. The close relationship between furniture makers and house builders increases the plausibility of such aesthetic influences.[2]

The tenons on the legs, the aprons, and on the four mortises on the top board for which the leg tenons are intended, are each marked by a carefully brushed character. Together the four characters read "yu zhou hong huang" (the universe is vast and time is eternal). This is the second sentence in the ancient and popular calligraphic exercise text *Qian Zi Wen* (Thousand-Character Essay). The first sentence of this text, "tian di xuan huang" (the heavens are dark and the earth is yellow), is commonly used in furniture making, either to mark the four legs of a chair or to distinguish between chairs or tables of a set. Often a pair of objects, such as tables at the Zi Jin An Nunnery in Dongshan, Suzhou county, is marked with *tian* and *di* (heaven and earth). The marks assist the carpenter and any later reassembler in constructing the object. The *Qian Zi Wen* essay first became popular among calligraphers during the Sui period (581–618) and was still commonly practiced, as well as published, during the Ming period.[3] Large tables with everted flanges are often marked, perhaps because they were easily disassembled and the placement of the legs easily confused, or because they were important pieces of furniture.

Yang Zheng Tu Jie (Illustrations and Descriptions of Proper Upbringing), 1594 edition.

Construction

The top of the table is one solid board. Separate endpieces, which prevent the unattractive and easily split end grain from being exposed, are fit on either end with a mitered blind mortise-and-tenon join. The upper part of these endpieces are carved into everted flanges. At each of the four ends of the long surfaces of the top board is what appears to be an octagonal, filled mortise, one and one-half inches in width. It is possible that a wooden dowel, or, as one person has postulated, a tube of sand or lead, was placed within the wood blank to keep it from torquing.[4] Another solid-top table of similar length and size belongs to David Hill Asian Art, San Francisco. It has similarly shaped, filled mortises in the same position suggesting that they were structural and not blemishes.

The four legs all blind double tenon into the top board. The apron, with high-relief decoration, passes through each leg in an elongated bridle join. The two legs at either end sit on a foot base that is rounded at the front and rear. To further rein-

force the solidity of the legs, a decorative panel with pierced carving is fit into the spaces between the two legs at either end. A stretcher above the panel tenons into either leg. Small blind tenons join the panel to the legs, the stretcher above it, and the foot base below.

1. Li Yu, "Duo Jin Lou" (The First Prize Tower), in *Li Liweng Xiaoshuo Shiwu Zhong* (Fifteen Stories of Li Liweng). Hangzhou: Zhejiang Renmin Chubanshe, 1983, p. 173.

2. The carpenters' manual, the *Lu Ban Jing,* contains instructions on both architecture and furniture construction, which also share common construction techniques.

3. Research for this exhibition revealed that the *Qian Zi Wen* was not the only source for marking furniture. On an immense *tieli* table with everted flanges in an American collection are found the four characters "Kong ren da shang," which could be interpreted as "the great man Confucius [or surnamed Kong] is superior." Another *huanghuali* table of similar construction, with everted flanges, in the same collection has three of its four corners marked with the characters "Huang da ren," meaning "the great person Huang [or yellow]." Presumably the *shang* (superior) character is implied. The characters seem to be praises or wishes for either the tables' patrons or deities.

4. As discussed with David Hill on August 15, 1995, concerning his table.

20. Side Table with Waist
[*tiaozhuo*] 黃花梨 條桌
33 in. (h) × 72 in. (w) × 28 in. (d)

Huanghuali

Wei Guo went out to the courtyard again, picked a stem of peonies, put it in the vase and placed it on the table [zhuo], *saying: "Now this is properly marrying—with flowers and candles!"*[1]

This table exhibits the elegance that can arise from satisfying proportions and simple details on a plain, functional form. It was of such elegance that Ming aestheticians seemed to be speaking when they used the word *su* (plain). Bold braces, strong hipped shoulders, and the short, and unusually cleft, hoof feet provide a sense of strength without heaviness—an aesthetic balance pursued by Ming craftsmen.

Simple, flat-ended (*pingtou*—without flanges) tables such as this one appear often in late-Ming woodblock prints and paintings. Like many tables and seats in China, they do not have one specific use, but are multifunctional. They may be placed against walls to hold decorative objects such as vases, rocks, bronzes, or candlesticks, providing a modest but elegant setting for the objects. Or, as other prints and paintings demonstrate, they may have been used for dining, studying, playing the *qin,* or for women to use as surfaces for sewing. Characters in novels often instruct servants to carry over a table for this use or that, confirming the understanding of the impermanent placement and multiple functions of Chinese furnishings in a room. (The movability of furniture in early Western households is reflected in the French word *meubles*—movables—to distinguish furniture from immobile property such as land and houses.)

The braces that extend from the inside corners of the legs to the underside of the tabletop, giving the table extra support and stability, are often seen on tables in late-Ming woodblock prints. In current terminology, they are called *bawang cheng*, a term frequently translated as "giant's arm brace." (A *bawang* is in fact a hegemonist, and the term *hero's brace* may be more appropriate. This term also expresses the impression of extra strength that these braces add to a table. However, since "giant's arm brace" has already become part of English vocabulary, I hesitate to change it.)

The braces on this table are particularly unusual. On most tables, the braces are made of one or two pieces of wood fashioned into an S-curve and attached to the closest batten under the table. Each of the braces on this table, however, is composed of three pieces of wood, preventing the presence of crossgrain at the curvature, which would weaken the brace. Moreover, the braces are more angular, affording the table a stronger appearance.

Construction
The tabletop is formed of four mitered mortise-and-tenon-joined frame members, with tenons exposed on the sides, within which floats a single panel that is slipped into grooves on the shorter frame members. On the underside of the tabletop are four battens, blind butt tenoning into one framework; these fit into sliding dovetail grooves on the floating panel. The tabletop frame members rest on the waist and apron, which are carved from one piece of wood.

The square-section legs double tenon into the tabletop frame members, in an embracing shoulder tenon with a tapered dovetail wedge. The hanger tenon of the aprons then slides over dovetail housing and locks into place.

Giant's arm braces extend from each of the legs to the underside of the table. The two at each end cross each other, the top one slipping into a slot within and hooking over the lower one. Both slip into slots on the slightly thickened batten as well as attach to the underside of the floating panel. These braces are unusual in several manners. Each is made of three pieces of wood joined to each other by through tenons. This way the grain is always straight and the brace is not in danger of breaking on the grain. Moreover, they cross in the above-stated manner with the lower brace thickening at the point where it attaches straight onto the panel of the tabletop. The original ramie and lacquer on the underside of the table are intact.

The square-section legs end in low horse-hoof feet.

1. Tianran Chisou, p. 180.

Nan Pipa Ji (The Southern Story of the Lute), Wanli Qifengguan edition.

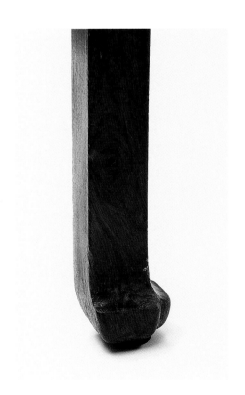

21. Square Table [*fangzhuo*] 黃花梨 方桌

33 in. (h) × 39 in. (w) × 38 in. (d)
Huanghuali

Zhoude quickly bought a fish, a pig's foot, fresh fruit, and a large bottle of wine, brought it home and called to the maid Chunmei to make preparations, adding that it was already the shen hour! [2:00—4:00 P.M.] *His wife moved out the table [zhuo]. Liang Gong and his wife sat down and Zhoude and his wife sat across from them. The maid poured the wine and the four drank.*[1]

Chunmei closed the door, put a square table in the center of the room, and brought out wine and food. Jingjin and his wife, shoulder to shoulder, and folding their legs, sat down....They ate for a while and then the chessboard was brought out and the three played chess.[2]

The square table was a standard piece of domestic furniture. A table in this shape was particularly convenient for eating in casual circumstances. Woodblock prints reveal that, at elegant gatherings, each person ate at his or her own table, or two people sat at one table, both seated on the same side of the table. In such situations the table was usually rectangular in shape and each person was given his own group of dishes. In a more informal setting, friends or relatives sat together at one table and took morsels from common dishes placed in the center. On a square table the centrally placed food is comfortably equidistant from all diners.

As has been pointed out previously, few pieces of Chinese furniture were reserved for explicit functions. A table used for serving food at mealtime could also be the surface for a chess game or fortune telling several hours later. Illustrations for *Jin Ping Mei* and *Shui Hu Zhuan* depict square tables being used for these multiperson activities as well as for group meals, as seen in the illustration for the round-back chair (cat. 11).

In its structure, this table combines the two distinct Chinese table-construction techniques—waisted and recessed-leg—identified by Wang Shixiang. Tables with waists usually have square legs and hoofed feet. Round legs appear primarily on tables with recessed legs and no waist. This table, interestingly, has both a waist and round-section legs that go straight down to the

floor. Such composites are not common, but a rectangular table of similar construction is depicted in an illustration for the late-sixteenth-century collection of exemplary-hero tales, *Yang Zheng Tu Jie*.

Construction
The tabletop is constructed of four frame members, mitered and through tenoned, surrounding a two-panel top surface slipped into a tongue-and-groove on two opposite sides. The two panels themselves are joined at the center by a small mortise-and-tenon join. Two battens, dovetailed into the bottom of the panels, maintain the level of the top surface. Shrinkage of the center panels created a gap that has since been filled by a thin strip of wood.

The top rests on the waist and apron, which are constructed of a single piece of wood, and on the four round legs. The rounded legs have a tapered dovetail wedge over which the apron slides and into which it locks with through-dovetail housing, meeting the leg with a mitered edge. The aprons have been pinned to the legs. For additional support, below the apron are rounded, two-piece, humpback stretchers, mitered blind tenoning into the legs; at their central, higher sections of the humpback, the stretchers abut the apron. Sliding keys are dovetailed onto each apron and lock the apron and waist to the tabletop. To ensure further that the legs do not slip outward, giant's arm braces reach between the legs, into which they are tenoned, and the battens below the table-top, where they are nailed.

Feng Yue Zheng Qi, 1620 edition.

1. Feng Menglong (1574–1646), "Ren Xiaozi Lie Xing Wei Shen" (Filial Mr. Ren via Martyrdom Becomes a Deity). In *Yu Shi Ming Yan* (Clear Words to Instruct the World [c. 1627]). Reprint. Hong Kong: Zhong Hu Shu Ju, 1978, pp. 571–86.

2. *Jin Ping Mei,* 1618. Reprint. *Jin Ping Mei Ci Hua.* Taibei: Zeng Ni Zhi Wenhua Shiye Youxian Gongci, 1982, chapter 83, p. 266.

22. Table with Lotus-leaf Waist
[*banzhuo*] 黃花梨 半桌

33 in. (h) × 42 in. (w) × 22 in. (d)
Huanghuali

The room on the left was the principal courtesan's bedroom. In the center was a guest's seat, above which hung a landscape by a famous artist. On the incense table was an ancient bronze [boshan] censer, in which cakes of ambergris were burning On either side of the room was a table [shu zhuo] on which were arranged some antiques.[1]

The rectangular shape and the size of this table comprise common and convenient dimensions for tables in the traditional Chinese household. Such a table could easily be lifted from a position at the side of a room, where it may have displayed antiques, and moved to a bedside or windowside spot, where a meal or wine could be served.

This particular table exemplifies how highly skilled craftsmen of the late Ming, though staying within prescribed sizes and shapes, occasionally went far beyond practical and classical concerns to produce embellished, yet still classically refined, pieces of furniture.

The structures of this table are all derived from classical Chinese designs, but the cabinetmaker took great creative liberty in executing the piece. Several unusual features distinguish this table from others: (1) the legs begin as short cabriole legs at their uppermost sections, then extend downward as round legs from the apparent foot, to end in bulging, drum-stool-shaped feet; (2) dragon-shaped spandrels stretch diagonally from each leg to the carved-relief aprons; and (3) a thin waist, fabricated from a separate piece of wood, attached to the apron by hidden bamboo pins, is carved into an undulating band that resembles the edge of a pie crust or a lotus leaf.

The combination of these three features—the legs, the spandrels, and the waist—appear on one other known table, which is in the Wang Shixiang collection, now at the Shanghai Museum.[2] The sizes of these tables match almost exactly. The uniqueness of their features and the similarity of their sizes suggest that both tables may have been products of the same workshop, and possibly were originally a pair. While many pairs of chairs have remained together, most tables have been separated. A pair of Ming, square *huang-huali* tables may be seen at the Zi Jin An Nunnery in Dongshan, Suzhou county. Inscriptions under each table in the pair mark one as *tian* (heaven) the other as *di* (earth). Unfortunately, the table in this exhibition has no such markings.

Two other tables, both in private American collections, display the same legs and feet and the lotus-leaf waist, but they have humpback stretchers instead of spandrels between the legs.

The short cabriole leg that extends into a circular-section leg is reminiscent of another table type, the lower, extended legs of which are detachable, thus permitting the upper section to be used as a *kang* table. Table-leg removal, like the collapsibility of Chinese folding chairs and tables, made moving the furniture easy and convenient. The leg on this table, however, is crafted of one piece of wood and is not detachable. Wang Shixiang has termed this type of leg *aizhuozhantuishi* (short-table, extended-leg style).[3] A Yuan painting, *Xiao Xia Tu* (Relieving the Summer Heat),[4] depicts a similar table, but the extended leg below the pseudo-short-cabriole leg is square rather than circular in section.

The elegance of this table derives from its overall form and its many finely wrought details. The elegant, undulating waistband and the animated spandrels are accompanied by delicate, carved decorations on the aprons. Those on the long side display relief carvings of phoenixes facing a sun (*shuangfeng chaoyang*), a metaphor suggesting that a time of high talents has arrived.[5] Wang Shixiang notes that the carving of birds and flowers on the shorter aprons on his table, which is identical to the carving on this table, resembles Wanli porcelain and he dates the table to that period. The carved lotus-leaf waist is comparable to rims on some Yuan and Ming porcelain vases. While no woodblock prints or paintings bear illustrations of the lotus-leaf edge or the drum-stool-shaped feet of this table, certain Wanli prints do depict an equal amount of dainty carving and detail demonstrating that this style existed at that time.

Construction
The tabletop is constructed of four mitered and through tenoned frame members and a floating panel fit into grooves in the frame members. Around the perimeter of the tabletop is a raised-edge *lanshuixian*, a water-restraining line. Most *lanshuixian* are carved out of the tabletop frame members. However, the lip on this table is composed of four strips of wood held in place by glue. While the lip is not a new or recent addition, wear and stains beneath the strip reveal that it was also not original to the table. At some point, perhaps in the eighteenth or nineteenth century, repairs were made to the table—some of the spandrels are old replacements, for example—and the owner may have requested that a *lanshuixian* be affixed at that time. Three battens below the tabletop are dovetailed onto the floating panel and tenoned into the frame members in order to keep the panels from warping. The two outer battens through tenon and are exposed. The lotus-leaf-shaped carved waist below the tabletop is attached by bamboo pins to the tabletop above and the apron below. The four legs, which, at the top, are cabriole shaped on their outer surfaces, but round in the interior, double tenon into the tabletop frame members, in an embracing shoulder tenon with a tapered dovetail wedge. The hanger tenon of the relief-carved aprons with cusped outlines then slides over dovetail housing and locks into place.

Giant's arm braces, with decorative carving in the shape of *lingzhi* fungus, extend from the legs to the battens on the underside of the tabletop, giving the table extra support and stability. Eight additional spandrels, carved in the shape of dragons—two for each leg—stretch from the legs to the aprons to further strengthen the table.

From the terminus of the short cabriole portion of the leg, a leg that is completely circular in section continues downward until it ends in the drum-stool-shaped foot.

1. Feng Menglong (1574–1646), "Mai You Lang Du Zhan Hua Kui" (The Oil Seller Alone Monopolizes the Principal Courtesan). In *Gudai Baihua Duanpian Xiaoshuo Xuan*, p. 257.

2. Wang Shixiang, *Connoisseurship of Chinese Furniture*, vol. 1, p. 172.

3. Ibid.

4. *Liang Song Minghua Ce* (Album Paintings of the Northern and Southern Dynasties). Beijing: Wenwu Chubanshe, 1963, plate 60.

5. *Cihai*. Shanghai: Shanghai Cishu Chubanshe, 1979, p. 341.

23. Incense Table [*xiangji*] 黃花梨 香几

30¾ in. (h) × 20 in. (w) × 20 in. (d)
Huanghuali

Ximen Qing was not yet aware of the situation. He just saw the maid Little Jade set out the incense table. In a little while, the Moon Lady, adjusting her clothes, came out and burned incense in the middle of the court. Then she bowed low toward the heavens and prayed.[1]

Chinese were burning woods to create fragrant odors at least as early as the Western Han period. Both secular and religious spaces—imperial offices and domestic chambers as well as places of worship—were graced with aromatics. About 180 B.C., Tang Huan, a mechanician in imperial employ, invented a censer known as a *boshan lu* (hill censer). This receptacle was crafted in the shape of a hill, and was often decorated with images of wild animals. *Boshan lu* were produced in both bronze and pottery.[2] The advent of censers gave rise to the necessity for an object on which to place them.

The earliest dated woodblock print, a frontispiece to the *Diamond Sutra* from 868, depicts the Buddha preaching; in front of him a large rectangular table holds offerings and, it appears, an incense burner. By the Song period, the incense burners in Buddhist woodblock prints—such as an illustrated edition of the *Guanyin Sutra* from 1240[3]—have been moved onto tall, thin tables with cabriole legs. Tables of similar dimensions supporting censers are also included in depictions of nonreligious events such as an outdoor gathering of men listening to a *qin* player in the Song painting *Listening to the Qin,* by the Song emperor Huizong (Palace Museum, Beijing).

The incense stand is one of the main table types listed in the *San Cai Tu Hui*, the late-Ming encyclopedia. During the Ming period it was probably a standard piece of furniture in any household that could afford the luxury. In the domestic setting, incense continued to be used for both secular and religious purposes. Woodblock prints and paintings of the period depict them in bedrooms, studies, and reception halls, offering the viewer an olfactory sense of the scene presented. These tables are shown in courtyards and gardens as well; they were often carried out of doors when obeisance was made to the heavens.

Unlike many furniture pieces, the incense table's name implies a specific use. Most furniture types in the late Ming period were multifunctional, and woodblock prints of the period demonstrate that these slender tables were not confined to the sole purpose of holding incense burners aloft. Flower vases and decorative rocks were also frequently displayed on incense tables.

The incense burner also differed from other tables because it was intended to be placed away from the wall, closer to the center of activity where it could spread its perfumed smoke. Because of this central position and the potential to be viewed from many directions, incense tables in general—whether they are round, hexagonal, square, or even multilobed—are symmetrical in shape.

Construction

The top is constructed of five rounded frame members, joined to each other with half-lapped scarf joins. A *lanshuixian* (water-restraining line), rims the entire top surface. A single circular panel floats in a groove within the frame members. The five bulging legs double tenon into the top frame members at the point of their joins, further securing the top. A five-piece waist is secured to the frame above and the apron below by dovetailed keys. Rounded and convex aprons with mitered edges slide over and tenon into the legs. The rounded horse-hoof feet at the bottom of the legs double tenon into a circular continuous stretcher, locking together the five frame members, which are held together by half-lapped scarf joins with pegs. The continuous stretcher secures the entire construction. Five additional low feet double tenon into the continuous stretcher, thus thwarting its deterioration from ground moisture and covering the joint.

Xi Xiang Ji (Tale of the Western Chamber), Xiang Xue Ju edition, 1614.

1. *Jin Ping Mei,* in *Jin Ping Mei Ci Hua,* chapter 21, p. 293.

2. Silvio A. Bedini, *The Trail of Time.* Cambridge, Eng.: Cambridge University Press, 1994, p. 28.

3. Reprinted in Zhen Zhengduo, *Zhonggu Gudai Muke Hua Xuanji* (A Selection of Chinese Ancient Woodblock Prints). Beijing: Ren Min Meishu Chubanshe, 1984, vol. 2.

24. Incense Table [*xiangji*] 黃花梨 香几

36 in. (h) × 20 in. (w) × 20 in. (d)
Pine with polychrome lacquer

Yingying: "Hongniang, don't tell my mother about it. It is getting to be dusk; go and arrange the table for the incense burner. We'll go to the garden to burn incense....

"Hongniang, open the side door, and take out the table for the incense burner....Move it near the Taihu rocks."[1]

The imagery detailed in colored and carved lacquer on the surface of this incense stand portrays a pair of egrets standing among lotus leaves, buds, and blossoms. This design represents a wish for successfully passing the civil exams and becoming an official. Because the Chinese language has an extraordinary number of homophones, many Chinese decorative symbols act as rebuses. The significance of the image depicted here derives from the expression "yi lu lian ke," meaning "the whole way successively passing the *ke* [a section of the exam]," which is homophonic with the words "an egret and a group of lotuses."

Flying in the air above the lotus and egret scene are two magpies, which symbolize double happiness, as the word for magpie, *xique* or *xi*, is homophonous with the word for happiness, *xi*.

Construction

The round top sits atop five vertical posts that descend to become the five legs of the table. Curved panels with pierced designs are located between the posts. Below the panels is a continuous, rounded, double-lobed apron. The five cabriole legs, which bulge out from the aprons, each have winglike decorations approximately halfway down. The legs end in small, spherical feet, which then curve back upward with leaflike flaps resting against the legs. The feet tenon in to a lower stand that, like the top of the incense stand, has a top resting on five vertical posts—each one directly below its corresponding upper foot. Between the posts are rounded, pierced panels and below them is a continuous, rounded, double-lobed apron. The complete stand rests on five small feet that

Huan Cui Tang Yuan Jing Tu (Scenes and Pictures of the Huan Cui Tang Garden), Wanli period.

are aligned with the vertical posts and legs above.

1. Wang Shifu (1271–1368), *Xi Xiang Ji* (Tale of the Western Chamber). In Ch'u Chai and Winberg Chai, trans. and ed., *A Treasury of Chinese Literature*. New York: Appleton-Century, 1965, p. 398.

25. *Kang* Table [*kangzhuo*] 黃花梨 炕桌

12½ in. (h) × 39 in. (w) × 24¾ in. (d)

Huanghuali

She arranged an unusual jasmine tea, vegetables, and treats all on a one-foot-high tray, placed it on the gold-lacquered kang table, and spread out the brocade rug. Then she called Fuqing to come sit on the southwestern kang, which in the past the family had reserved only for guests.[1]

The *kang* is a brick oven platform with a surface about three feet off the ground, which fills from a third to a half of the room and is built into many homes in northern China. Heating flues run within the *kang*, and during winter months most activities take place on this warmed surface. Low tables known as *kangzhuo* (*kang* tables), as well as small cabinets, sit on the *kang* for convenient use. Wang Shixiang has noted that southern homes, specifically in Suzhou, where much fine furniture was made during the late Ming period, did not have *kangs*, as winters there were not as harsh as those in the north and did not necessitate such intense heating methods. Small *kang* tables, however, occasionally were placed on beds and couch-beds.

Despite a paucity of imagery in Ming prints and paintings, the abundance of *kang* tables and the presence of extant *kang* in dwellings ranging from the imperial palace to rural peasant homes testify to their prevalence.

The *kang*, like the couch-bed, continued the seating postures of pre-chair China. Sitting on a *kang* was similar to being on a mat on the floor. If the sitters' legs were not hanging down the side of the *kang*, they were either folded in some manner, stretched out, or arranged in a kneeling position. A low table placed on a *kang* was a convenient working surface for painting, writing, sewing, or laying out food.

Construction

The top of the table is constructed of four mitered, mortise-and-tenoned frame members, within which float three panels. The tabletop rests on a waist, a long tenon on the bottom of which sits in a groove on the top of the apron. The serpentine-shaped legs have a tapered dovetail wedge over which the relief-carved and cusped-outline apron slides and into which it locks with through dovetail housing. The serpen-

tine legs double tenon into the tabletop and finish with lobed feet.

1. Meng Bisheng, *Jin Wu Meng* (Dream of the Gold Room; 1665). Reprint. Chengdu: Ba Shu Shushe, 1988, chapter 35, p. 275.

Jin Ping Mei, Chongzhen edition.

26. Round-corner Cabinet
[*gui, chu*] 黃花梨 桂，櫥

72 in. (h) × 33 in. (w) × 26 in. (d)
Huanghuali

Entering the first of three houses (which is large) it has therein some huge cupboards very well wrought and carved, but the work is more for strength and durability than for show. ... Their furniture is durable and of great repute and credit, which endures for their sons and grandsons.[1]

Homes of the Ming period did not have built-in closets, therefore cabinets, large and small, were a necessity for the storage of a wide variety of objects and the hiding of clutter from view while all those small essentials remained close at hand.

The seventeenth-century writer and decorator Li Yu (1611–80), in his *Xian Qing Ou Ji* (Notes Written in Moments of Idleness), discusses a variety of domestic furnishings. He notes in his essay on the cabinet that drawers and shelves are necessary to take the most advantage of a cabinet's space:

> In making a cabinet, there is no necessity for a clever scheme, only thought to determine how to store the greatest quantity of things. There are enormous cabinets that cannot store many things and that aren't as good as a cabinet that is small in size but has a spacious interior. A cabinet of small size but high capacity is excellent. Highly skilled carpenters are not the same as those with low skills, but those that can make a good one have no secret techniques. The interior just must have some boards and that's it. The largest cabinets should not have more than two, three or, at the most, four levels. If one level only necessitates the use of one level, then on one level put a few large and tall things, or, in the same vein, if there are many short, small things, put all the small, short things on one level. If below is filled but above is empty, is this not a waste of space? Then, on either side of each level, nail thin strips of wood and put on another board. The board does not have to be too wide—half or even a third the depth of the cabinet. When you need it, put it up; when you aren't using it, take it down....Now about drawers in the interior of a cabinet, you cannot have too many. The more the better. Each drawer can further be divided into

compartments for placing different types of things....So by dividing each cabinet interior into many shelves, and each drawer into many small units, the energy spent on finding things and organizing things can be lessened. With the time saved one can read books and write essays.[2]

That Li Yu feels compelled to mention the usefulness of shelves and drawers suggests that many cabinets at the time did not possess these convenient amenities. Drawers, however, were not a seventeenth-century invention. They can be seen on a lacquer box at the Shoso-in dating from the Tang period (618–907). The cabinet pictured here originally had two shelves, a detachable one above (now replaced) and the other, permanent, serving as the upper casing of two side-by-side drawers.

Construction

Four frame members with through mitered tenons, exposed on the sides, surround a floating panel to create the top of the cabinet. Two supporting transverse braces under the floating panel tenon into the front and back frame members. The four round, vertical posts at each corner of the cabinet tenon through the top frame members.

The two side panels of the cabinet float in grooves on the front and back posts, and each is additionally secured by two transverse braces, which blind tenon into the front and back posts. At the top of the panel a stretcher dovetails onto the front and back posts, and wraps over the top of the panel. A bottom stretcher through tenons into the front and back posts and has a groove to accept the floating panel. Under the stretcher is a curved apron with attached spandrels, which sits in a groove on either post.

The doors are constructed of four frame members, joined by mitered mortise-and-tenon. A floating panel sits in grooves in the frame members, and is further supported by two battens attached by sliding dovetails on the interior of the panels. The outer frame members of the door extend past the top rail at top and bottom. These round tenons serve as pivots. Above they fit into a hole on the underside of the frame member of the cabinet's top, and, below, into a protruding

Zhongyi Shui Hu Zhuan (The Water Margin), Wanli edition.

stretcher below the door opening. Between the two doors is a removable vertical stile that tenons into the frame member above. A groove across half of the lower end of the stile slides over a tenon on the protruding stretcher below the doors.

The back panel of the cabinet is constructed of four boards, supported by three transverse braces, attached by sliding dovetails, and sitting in grooves on the vertical posts. The bottom stretcher blind mortise-and-tenons into the back posts.

The entire interior of the cabinet is coated with a thick yellow lacquer. Inside the cabinet, four front-to-back braces blind tenon into the lowest front and back stretchers. A board sits atop these braces creating the cabinet's bottom. A shelf rests on the upper transverse braces and a lower shelf sits on the lower transverse braces.

1. Portuguese Dominican Gaspar da Cruz (1556), as quoted in C.R. Boxer, *South China in the Sixteenth Century*, p. 106.

2. Li Yu, *Xian Qing Ou Ji* (Notes Written in Moments of Idleness). Translation by this author.

27. Pair of Round-corner Cabinets
[*gui, chu*] 黃花梨紫檀 桂，櫉

72 in. (h) × 33 in. (w) × 26 in. (d)

Huanghuali, zitan

They were led through the inner doors, each more magnificent than the last. There were forty maids, standing in the courtyard, and twenty servants, leading them to the east hall, where they found a great display of rare and precious objects. There were many fine chests, cupboards,…mirrors and trinkets such as one would not expect to find in this world.[1]

Like the standard table form, this cabinet type was produced by carpenters in a variety of materials, for a range of patrons. For humbler homes, the round-cornered cabinet was made in softwoods, such as elm, and often coated with lacquer; for more affluent households the form was elaborated by being executed in either fine hardwoods or intricately carved cinnabar lacquer.[2] A further variation on the theme is black lacquered with spattered mica (private collection, Boston). This pair of cabinets, while very similar to the previous standard, round-cornered example, still maintains both individual aesthetic as well as structural differences.

A subtle but luxurious element of these taller-than-standard cabinets is the use of *zitan* wood for the four corner posts. In late-Ming China, the dark—almost black—and tight-grained *zitan* was the most preferred and hardest of woods. A *zitan pipa* (lute) and a chessboard stored at the Shoso-in in Japan testify to the fact that as early as the Tang period the Chinese prized this wood: The pairing of *zitan* and *huanghuali* is rare but not unique.

In addition to the incorporation of *zitan*, two structural elements distinguish this pair of cabinets from the previous one: an extra horizontal panel below the cabinet doors, which allows for more storage space, and the absence of a center stile between the doors. Central stiles, as can be seen on the cabinet in catalogue number 26, originally functioned to add support to the top horizontal frame members when the doors were open. If the stile were not present, the top frame member could sink down a bit, making the doors difficult to reclose. The stile could be removed to accommodate placement of large objects inside the cabinet. The central stile exists on the Tang-period cabinets in

the Shoso-in, but by the end of the Ming period, some carpenters had already devised cabinets that did not require them.

Construction

Four frame members with through mitered tenons, exposed on the sides, surround a floating panel to create the top of the cabinet. Two supporting transverse braces under the floating panel tenon into the front and back frame members. The four round, vertical posts at each corner of the cabinet, all with a double beaded molding, tenon through the top frame members.

The two side panels of the cabinet float in grooves on the front and back posts; each is additionally secured by two transverse braces that blind tenon into the front and back posts. At the top of the panel, a stretcher dovetails onto the front and back posts and wraps over the top of the panel. A bottom stretcher, with a double beaded molding, through tenons into the front and back posts and has a groove to accept the floating panel. The exposed tenons' ends are shaped to match the molded beading on the posts. Under the stretcher is a curved apron with attached spandrels that sits in a groove on either post.

The doors are constructed of four frame members with beaded moldings, joined by mitered mortise-and-tenon. A floating panel sits in grooves of the frame members and is further supported by two battens attached by sliding dovetails on the interior of the panels. The outer frame members of the door extend at the top and bottom past the top rail. These round tenons are pivots and, above, fit into a hole on the underside of the frame member of the cabinet's top and, below, into a protruding stretcher below the door opening. Under this protruding stretcher are two side-by-side floating panels, separated by a vertical divider tenoning into the top and bottom stretchers. These panels create a deep supplementary storage compartment within the cabinet.

The back panel of the cabinet is constructed of four boards, supported by three transverse braces, attached by sliding dovetails, and sitting in grooves on the vertical posts. The bottom stretcher blind mortise-and-tenons into the back posts.

Inside the cabinet four front-to-back braces blind tenon into the lowest front and back stretchers. A board sits atop these braces creating the cabinet's bottom. At the center of the cabinet, a two-drawer unit rests on the transverse braces on the interior of the side panels. A top shelf rests on the upper transverse braces and a lower shelf sits on the lower transverse braces. This last shelf is level with the front protruding stretcher, thus making a hidden compartment in the area below.

1. Du Guanting (850–933), "Qiuxu Ke zhuan" (The Curly-Bearded Guest). Trans. from *A Treasury of Chinese Literature*, p. 118.

2. Such as a dated (1585), Wanli reign period example at the Österreichisches Museum für angewandte Kunst, Vienna, that is 67 cm high. It is published in Beurdeley, *Chinese Furniture*, p. 102.

28. Bookcase [*shujia, shuge*] 黃花梨 書架，書格

72 in. (h) × 33¾ in. (w) × 16 in. (d)
Huanghuali with fir shelves

Whenever there's a recess from court, his hand never rests from turning the pages of his books.... His bright window is wonderfully clear; his desk cleared, for study, is perfectly neat. The bright window is wonderfully clear; incense smoke wafts by the green gauze curtains.... If you were to count up his books, the number would exceed forty thousand.... Rue-scented leaves have chased away all bookworms from his pages.[1]

With the development and spread of printing, which had begun in the Tang period, books became more readily available. By the late Ming, books not only were the mark of an educated man, they had become an easily obtainable status symbol. Displaying such symbols, therefore, was also essential.

Primarily books, and some scrolls, can be seen on the shelves of bookcases in late-Ming woodblock prints. The scrolls would be laid horizontally on the shelves, their round ends pointing out. Books were stored flat on their sides on these shelves, their covers facing up; they were not placed standing upright on their spines as in Europe.

During the Song, books were bound with hardcovers. At that time, they were stored with the bound edge facing up and the mouth of the book on the surface of the shelf.[2] By the Ming period, bookbinding formats had radically changed. Books had softcovers and placing them upright would have damaged their pages, thus storing methods had to be altered as well. If one were to look at a filled Ming bookcase, only the bottoms of the pages would have been visible, not, as in Europe, title-inscribed spines. Wooden title tags, which would assist in a book search, were often attached to the books by strings.

Construction

The top frame is constructed of four rounded members; the side members meet the front and rear posts with mitered mortise-and-tenons, with only the side tenons exposed. The panel is flat on the bottom but slightly beveled toward the edge to allow it to slip into grooves in the members along its four sides.

Lie Nu Zhuan (Biographies of Exemplary Women), Wanli edition.

Two battens cross the top of the case and are joined to the panel with a sliding dovetail pin, keeping the shelf flat. These battens are on the bottom of all the other shelves, where they are not visible.

The frame members of all the shelves except the top miter through tenon to the posts and are exposed on the front and sides.

Both of the top two shelves have galleries constructed of thinner horizontal rails attached by mitered mortise-and-tenon joints, and are reinforced with pairs of vertical braces.

Below the center shelf are two drawers separated by a vertical divider, which miter blind tenon into a lower frame member. Below the bottom shelf are aprons on all four sides that are constructed of three parts joined together by a half-lapped, mitered join and fitted into grooves on the posts. There are traces of lacquer on the bottoms of the shelves. All members are round.

1. From *Pipa Ji* by Gao Ming (1305-?). Translation from Jean Milligan, *The Lute*. New York: Columbia University Press, 1980, p. 251.

2. Edward Martinique, *Chinese Traditional Bookbinding*. Taibei: Chinese Materials Center, 1983.

29. Garment Rack [*yijia*] 黃花梨 衣架

72 in. (h) × 81 in. (w) × 18 in. (d)

Huanghuali

A few steps farther on was a neat bamboo hedge, on the other side of which, towards the north, he found a small house. ... The door was barred by a garment rack, on which was hanging an embroidered petticoat; and on seeing this, Wang stepped back, knowing that he had walked into the ladies' quarters. But his presence had already been noticed inside.[1]

Since Chinese architecture did not accommodate room for closets, garment racks, along with cabinets, became essential furnishings for the bedroom at an early date. Woodblock prints and paintings show that clothing was tossed over these racks rather than laid out in any particular or neat manner. One late-Ming woodblock depicts a couple suspended in an erotic encounter upon the garment rack[2] but, beyond that one instance, it seems garment racks were among the few pieces of furniture that had a specific and singular function.

Like the bed and other bedroom furniture, the garment rack was probably often part of a dowry gift and appropriately decorated. Few seventeenth-century *huanghuali* garment racks are extant and each has its own distinctive decoration. Few are as elaborately carved as this example, however.

The carving on this garment rack displays an array of good wishes. First and foremost, in the central panel, are representations of blessings—prosperity, rank, and longevity, known in Chinese as *fu, lu* (literally an official's salary), and *shou*, respectively. Here the concepts are depicted as three men known as the Three Stars: Laozi, the older man with the enlarged forehead, holding a peach, represents *shou*. A gentleman scholar symbolizes *fu,* and a high official signifies *lu*, the prestigious rank and the high salary that accompanies a government post. The Three Stars stand within a landscape of bamboo, pine, and plum blossom, the grouping known as "the three friends of winter" (see cat. 12), which was also a popular motif in the late Ming.

The personification of these three wishes existed in Chinese art as early as the late Yuan period. In the late-Ming and early Qing periods, when this piece was produced, the three characters were still

popular, appearing on textiles, ceramics, and woodblock prints as well as many paintings.[3]

Both side panels depict pairs of mythical phoenixes, the highest-ranking species among birds. The phoenixes are perched on rocks, surrounded by peonies, which are considered the king of flowers and are symbolic of rank and wealth. The spandrels of the rack are all decorated with dragons, the most prestigious of all creatures.

The carving on this garment rack is similar to that on a washbasin stand in the Wang Shixiang collection, which shows a child riding a *qilin*; it is one of the few examples of Ming furniture that bears carved figures. Both of these pieces have similar decorative, three-"toed" marks on the hills, probably representing grass or flowers. The style of the carving places the piece in the second half of the seventeenth century.

The garment rack was brought to the United States by Mrs. May Smith, a missionary who lived in China for many years during the early part of this century. She spoke Chinese, and was friendly with members of the imperial family. According to family lore, princesses gave the garment rack to her as a gift.

Construction

The rack has suffered some damage and been repaired over the years. The central panel was broken and reglued. The lowest horizontal bar must at some point have come loose from its tenons on either side. With the original mortises destroyed, the restorers moved the bar up three inches and carved out new mortises. The old ones were filled. One spandrel below the upcurved end is a replacement. Two other spandrels, which would have served to support the bar under the central three panels, have been lost. Despite the losses to the rack, its delicate and elaborate carving make it a rare piece. There are very few examples of *huanghuali* garment racks, as they are fragile and it is unlikely that many have survived.

A bar with beaded edges and a central bead forms the top rail. Carved dragon heads made of separate pieces of wood tenon into either end of the top rail. The right dragon head is a replacement. The two square vertical posts miter tenon into

Xi Xiang Ji (Tale of the Western Chamber), Xiang Xue Ju edition, 1614.

the top rail. Carved, pierced spandrels depicting dragons tenon into the top rail and the vertical posts. On either side of the inner surface of the central section of the vertical posts is an additional, shorter, square, vertical bar with lotus buds carved at the upper ends. The top and bottom rails of the central-panel construction miter mortise-and-tenon through the vertical lotus-bud bars and secure them to the longer vertical posts. Two shorter vertical dividers miter mortise-and-tenon into these central horizontal bars to create spaces for the three carved, pierced panels. The panels float in grooves on the dividers. Spandrels, now no longer extant, once provided extra support below the lower bar. At either end, an additional horizontal stretcher miter through tenons into the lower part of the vertical lotus-bud bars to further secure them. Carved, pierced spandrels depicting dragons tenon into this stretcher and the vertical posts. The vertical posts butt tenon into the foot bases, which are carved with front and back drums. Carved, pierced spandrels depicting dragons tenon into the vertical posts and the foot base, in the front and the back, to maintain the stability of the vertical posts.

1. From Pu Songling (c. 1620–90), *Liao Zhai Zhi Yi* (1679).
Trans. based on Herbert A. Giles, "The Boat-girl Bride," in
Strange Stories from a Chinese Studio. Shanghai: Kelly and
Walsh, 1908, p. 355.

2. In *Hua Ying Jin Zhen* (Variegated Positions of the
Flowery Battle), reprinted in Robert van Gulik, *Erotic
Colour Prints of the Ming Period*. Tokyo: Private edition,
1951.

3. See Anne Burkus-Chasson's catalogue entries in *New
Interpretations of Ming and Qing Paintings*. Shanghai: Shuhua
Chubanshe, 1994, p. 53.

Furniture from the Ming-period Tomb of Pan Yunzheng

30a. Alcove Bed

14 in. (h) × 12⅛ in. (w) × 10¹⁵⁄₁₆ in. (d)
This covered bed with encircling railings, supporting posts, and a hanging curtain is modeled after the architecture of open halls and corridors.

Six posts—one at each of the four corners and two at the front of the bed—are connected by a low lattice rail formed of *wan* (swastika-shaped) designs. The matting is made up of two layers—the lower layer of palm fiber, the upper of rattan. Below the waist is a "straight apron," which joins with the legs. The feet of the legs are shaped like horses' hoofs. The four posts at the front are also connected on either side by latticework fences of swastika-shaped designs. The four legs of the bed, from its "roof" downward, are planted on the bottom boards, while the top board serves as a "hat." The bottom supporting board is fitted to the sides by wedges. The posts are fitted into the lower edges, which are supported by twelve square feet, evenly distributed to support the weight. The top board is encircled by a protective lattice with crab apple design. A stool stands at the foot of the bed to assist a person while getting in and out of bed. While enormous in size, the whole bed is so constructed as to present an appearance of dainty lightness.

30b. Daybed

3⅛ in. (h) × 10½ in. (w) × 1¹⁵⁄₁₆ in. (d)
The daybed is supported by a frame that is fitted together with mitered corners. The upper layer within the frame is rattan; the lower layer is palm fiber. Below the frame, the waist and apron are constructed of a single piece of wood. The short legs terminate in feet of a square, horse-hoof shape.

30c. Cabinet

9 in. (h) × 5¾ in. (w) × 2⅞ in. (d)
This cabinet has wooden hinges and rounded corners. The feet of the cabinet, which are round on the outside and squared off on the inside, splay outward. The hardware is fitted at the top with a knob on which to hang a lock, while pulls are suspended at the bottom. The sides of the cabinet are constructed of one board that is fitted in a groove on the legs. The interior is fitted with a shelf that divides the cupboard into upper and lower sections. The lower part of the cupboard is

also fitted with an apron. Seen as a whole, the shape and design of the cupboard are unpretentious, comprised of clear and simple lines, conveying a sense of solidity. It is typical of Ming furniture.

30d. Painting Table

5½ in. (h) × 11¹¹⁄₁₆ in. (w) × 11¹¹⁄₁₆ in. (d)
The table is of a standard and proper style of the period. The frame members of the tabletop are joined together with mitered corners. A single wooden board is fitted within the frame. The rounded feet splay outward slightly. Two stretchers connect the two legs at either end.

30e. Long Table

5½ in. (h) × 10⅜ in. (w) × 4⅛ in. (d)
The four frame members of this table's top are mitered and tenoned together. A single board is fitted within the frame. The waist and apron are constructed of one piece of wood. The shortish feet end in square horse-hoof shapes that turn in slightly.

30f. Rectangular Table

5⅟₁₆ in. (h) × 7¹³⁄₁₆ in. (w) × 5½ in. (d)
The four frame members of this table's top are mitered and tenoned together. A single board is fitted into a groove on the inside of the frame members. The frame is slightly higher than the board, which creates a slight drop between the tabletop and the frame. The waist and apron are formed of a single piece of wood. Straight legs end in low, horse-hoof-shaped feet, which are turned in slightly. This is a typical example of Ming-period furniture with horse-hoof-shaped feet.

30g. Chest Stand

2⅞₁₆ in. (h) × 4¹¹⁄₁₆ in. (w) × 3 in. (d)
This stand is similar in form to the painting table, however the top is fashioned from one piece of wood. Its four edges are painted black to make it appear as if the edges are fashioned out of mitered corners. The bottom is fitted with plain aprons. The rounded legs are slightly splayed and the stretchers on either side create an overall impression of simplicity.

30h. Chest (see 30g)

2¾ in. (h) × 4⁵⁄₁₆ in. (w) × 2¾ in. (d)
The wooden chest is rectangular in shape. The sides are fitted together with dovetail joins. All the hardwood fittings and pulls are rectangular. The back has two brass hinges. Both sides are fitted with U-shaped handles.

30i. Armchair

7¹¹⁄₁₆ in. (h); seat: 3¹⁵⁄₁₆ in. (w) × 3 in. (d)
This high-backed southern official's hat chair is made entirely of rounded members. The two rear stiles also splay outward slightly and continue down through the seat to become the two back legs. The two arms are turned outward somewhat and pipe join with the two posts in front. No connecting side posts are under the arms. The seat is made of woven rattan and has a supporting board underneath. The legs are strengthened by connecting stretchers; the two on either side are slightly higher than those at the front and the back. The front stretcher is slightly thicker, to support the foot. This kind of southern official's hat chair was very popular during the Ming period.

30j. Wooden Stand for Square Brazier

1¾ in. (h) × 4⅛ in. (w) × 3⅜ in. (d)
Shaped like a low stool, this stand is constructed with mitered corners and has a waist. The wooden frame is hollow at the center, leaving space to insert a charcoal burner. The aprons have a cusped outline. The legs are curved and the horse-hoof-shaped feet turn inward. The entire stand sits on a continuous stretcher.

30k. Garment Rack

10⅝ in. (h) × 9¾ in. (w) × 2½ in. (d)
This piece consists of a horizontal bar that is curved upward slightly at the ends. It is supported by two vertical bars. Within this frame are positioned two horizontal bars, with spandrels under both ends that keep these bars in place. At the bottom, the frame is kept in place by two horizontal bars placed side by side, linked together by short connecting bars. This bottom rack could hold shoes and keep them off the humid floor.

30n. Chamber Pot
2¼ in. (h) × 2¹⁵⁄₁₆ in. (diam.)
The vertical sides of this wide-rimmed chamber pot are held together by two brass belts. The bottom is supported by four small feet.

30l. Towel Rack
9⁵⁄₁₆ in. (h) × 3⅞ in. (w) × 1¹⁵⁄₁₆ in. (d)
The rack is comprised of a horizontal bar with a slight upward curve at each end. It is supported by two vertical bars and spandrels below them. A flat, wide bar between the foot base functions as a shoe rack.

30o. Wooden Basin
1⁹⁄₁₆ in.. (h) × 3¹⁵⁄₁₆ in. (diam.)
Like the chamber pot (cat. 30n), this basin has vertical sides and is wide-rimmed. The middle part is held together by two brass belts. This basin was used for washing feet.

30m. Six-legged Washbasin Stand
4⁵⁄₁₆ in. (h) × 3⅞ in. (diam.)
The legs and horizontal supports of this elaborately designed and constructed piece all consist of rounded members. The tops of the posts are carved into bird's-head shapes.

Index

Page numbers in *italics* refer to pages on which illustrations are found. Appropriate text may also be found on these pages. Page numbers in **boldface type** refer to catalogue entries.